THIS IS
CAPE TOWN

THIS IS
CAPE TOWN

David Biggs

STRUIK

Struik Publishers
(A member of The Struik Publishing Group (Pty) Ltd)
Cornelis Struik House, 80 McKenzie Street
Cape Town 8001

Reg. No. 54/00965/07

First published in 1993
Text © David Biggs 1993

Photographic credits
The following photographers kindly provided material for this
book. Copyright remains with the individual photographers
listed below, unless otherwise stated.
D Balfour: front cover middle, pages 22 (bottom), 31, 118,
142 (top), 152 (top). **H Brink**: pages 114-115. **G Cubitt**:
pages 32, 35, 62, 66, 93 (top right), 124, 126 (bottom),
131, 140, 145 (top). **C de Kock** (© Struik Image Library) 60,
63 (top). **J Haigh**: pages 11 (bottom), 67 (right). **L Hoffmann**:
(© Struik Image Library) pages 10 (bottom), 23 (top and
bottom right), 101, 105 (bottom), 138 (top). **A Johnson**:
63 (bottom). **C Paterson-Jones**: back cover right, pages
10 (middle), 34 (top), 39 (bottom), 88 (top), 100, 104 (top),
108. **W Knirr**: back cover left, pages 16, 37 (Photo Access),
38, 44, 51, 76-77(top), 80, 94, 96-97, 107, 110, 113, 116-
117, 154-155 (Photo Access). **P Pickford**: page 18 (top).
P Ribton: front cover (main photograph). **State Archives,
Cape Town**, E7 862: page 7. **D Steele**: (Photo Access) pages
18 (bottom), 122. **J Szymanowski**: pages 121,123; (© Struik
Image Library) pages 22 (top), 28, 42, 48, 52-53, 127, 128
(top), 129, 139. **E Thiel**: pages 27, 138 (middle left and bottom
right); (© Struik Image Library): front cover left, back cover
middle, pages 1, 8, 10 (top), 11 (top), 12-15, 17 (top), 19-21,
24-26, 30, 33, 34 (bottom), 36, 39 (top, middle), 40, 41, 43,
45-47, 49, 50, 54-59, 61, 67 (left), 70-71, 72-73, 74 (bottom),
75, 76 (bottom), 78-79, 81-82, 83 (top), 84-87, 88 (bottom),
89-92, 93 (top left, bottom), 95, 98-99, 102-103, 104
(bottom), 105 (top), 106, 109, 111-112, 119-120, 125,
126 (top), 128 (bottom), 130, 133-137, 141, 142 (middle and
bottom), 143, 144, 145 (bottom), 146-151, 152 (bottom),
153, 156-158. **M Turnbull** (© Neethlingshof Estate): pages
29, 132. **M van Aardt**: front cover right, pages 2-3, 4-5, 23
(top left), 64-65, 68-69, 74 (top). **P Wagner**: (Photo Access)
pages 17 (bottom), 77 (bottom), 83 (bottom)

Project co-ordinator Annlerie van Rooyen
Editor Pippa Parker
Designer and DTP make up René Greeff
Indexer Sandie Vahl
Cartographers L Chegwidden (page 6), A Gracie (page 9)
Reproduction by Unifoto (Pty) Ltd, Cape Town
Printed and bound by South China Printing Co. Ltd., Hong Kong

ISBN 1 86825 433 X

HALF-TITLE PAGE: *Flower sellers add brightness to the city all
year round.* **PREVIOUS PAGE:** *This view of the mountain from
Blouberg is probably the one most often seen on postcards
and calendars.* **OPPOSITE:** *The city nestles between the
mountain and the bay.*

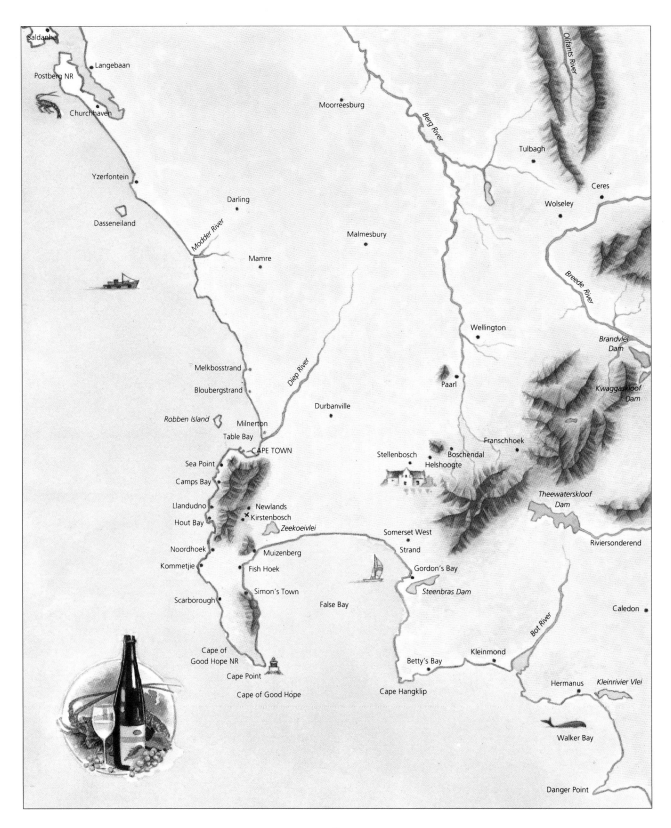

Saldanha
Langebaan
Postberg NR
Churchhaven
Yzerfontein
Dasseneiland
Moorreesburg
Olifants River
Berg River
Tulbagh
Ceres
Wolseley
Darling
Modder River
Malmesbury
Breede River
Mamre
Brandvlei Dam
Wellington
Melkbosstrand
Diep River
Paarl
Kwaggaskloof Dam
Bloubergstrand
Durbanville
Robben Island
Milnerton
Table Bay
Franschhoek
CAPE TOWN
Stellenbosch
Boschendal
Sea Point
Helshoogte
Camps Bay
Theewaterskloof Dam
Llandudno
Newlands
Kirstenbosch
Hout Bay
Zeekoeivlei
Somerset West
Riviersonderend
Noordhoek
Muizenberg
Strand
Kommetjie
Fish Hoek
Gordon's Bay
Scarborough
Simon's Town
Steenbras Dam
False Bay
Caledon
Cape of Good Hope NR
Bot River
Cape Point
Kleinmond
Betty's Bay
Cape of Good Hope
Hermanus
Kleinrivier Vlei
Cape Hangklip
Walker Bay
Danger Point

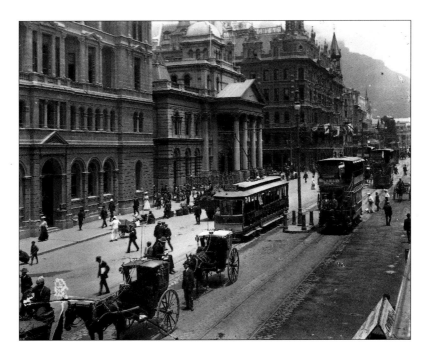

PROFILE OF CAPE TOWN

At midday the noon gun booms out over Cape Town, startling the pigeons into a flurry of wings in Greenmarket Square, and old Cape Town residents glance at their watches to check the time. It's a ritual that has lost its meaning in a world of digital watches and radio time-signals, but it is very much part of the changeless traditions of Cape Town, South Africa's oldest and most beautiful city.

Today there are no rock-breaking convicts in the harbour to sigh with relief and straighten their aching backs at the noon-day lunch signal. But Cape Town without the noon gun would be unthinkable. Time was vitally important to the sea captains of old who called in at Table Bay in the days of the three-masted sailing ships. They relied on such time checks in order to adjust the chronometers necessary for navigation. As part of the service provided at the harbour, a 'time ball' was constructed on the hill above the Table Bay Docks to signal the hour of one o'clock. It is still in action today. For the early European navigators to the Cape,

there were no such services at all, of course. They sailed into Table Bay after months at sea, in desperate need of provisions such as fresh water and meat, and wood for their galley stoves. They were met by small, yellow-skinned people who spoke in a strange, clicking manner and who were nicknamed *hottentotten*, meaning 'the stutterers', by the Dutch. These little people of the Cape traded cattle and sheep for iron knives, cooking pots and beads. After the establishment of the refreshment station at the Cape in 1652, voyagers also stocked up on supplies of Cape fruit and vegetables. And for more than three centuries, the Cape has continued to provide for the needs of visitors from all parts of the world, making it truly worthy of its title of 'Tavern of the Seas'.

The early history of the Cape is lost, for the simple reason that the first inhabitants did not leave any records, the only clues to their existence being rock paintings which tell us little about them. Although archaeologists can piece together a

picture of life at the Cape before European invasion, it is sketchy and, for the most part, inaccurate. This picture is of people who roamed the beaches – *strandlopers* – gathering food from the sea. There is also evidence of people inland who herded animals across large areas. They built no permanent houses and set up no towns. The Cape was also inhabited by wild animals no longer found here today: lions, elephants, hippos, rhino and buffalo. All have long since vanished in the wake of what we like to call 'civilization'.

But the beauty of Cape Town endures; in its mountains, its varied and spectacular coastline, its rich flora, and in much of its historic architecture; even modern development has evolved in response to the unique natural beauty here. No wonder Sir Francis Drake described this spot as 'the fairest Cape in all the circumference of the Earth'.

ABOVE: *In more leisurely times, tramcars and hansom cabs carried passengers along Adderley Street.*

TABLE MOUNTAIN

The old part of Cape Town lies in a great amphitheatre formed by the rocky sandstone masses of Table Mountain, Devil's Peak and Lion's Head. The mountain looms over the city, embracing it and providing Cape Town with a unique setting and character. Devil's Peak, to the left of the mountain when looking up from the city, gets its name from the legend of Van Hunks, the pirate, who met the Devil there for a smoking contest. As the two great smokers puffed their pipes, they formed the white table-cloth of cloud that is a regular feature of the mountain when the Cape south-easter blows. Lion's Head, at the other end of the mountain, might have been named because there were lions roaming there, but was more likely given its name simply because it looks rather like a lion, with the curved back and rump ending at Signal Hill, above Green Point.

On summer evenings powerful floodlights bathe the stone ramparts of the mountain in an eery blue light. In winter the slopes glisten with rain and mountain streams roar down the many narrow ravines, often carrying mudslides and trees in their path.

Hundreds of millions of years ago, when the Cape was part of the super-continent geologists call Gondwana, the feature that is now Table Mountain was a flat, empty plain. As the vast land-mass shifted and heaved, the plain slowly subsided under the sea. For 50 million years fine sediment built up, layer after layer. Then the earth's plates buckled again and the layers of sediment were thrust upward, first as an island and then, as the glaciers of the ice age tore and carved the solid mass, as what we now know as Table Mountain, Devil's Peak and Lion's Head. The layers of ancient submarine sediment can still be seen as horizontal lines across the face of the mountain.

The icy clouds of another cold front roll across the Cape.

More recently, the mountain and surrounding areas were the home of a rich variety of wild animals. Lions roamed the mountains, hippos wallowed in the swampy areas on the flats beneath the mountain. Most of the larger animals of Africa were found here, with one possible exception: the low fynbos vegetation was too short for giraffes.

Today almost all the wild animals have disappeared as man has encroached on their habitat. Only the smaller ones remain on the mountain – the little grysbok, porcupines, tortoises and the ubiquitous dassies, or rock rabbits.

An interesting addition to the mountain fauna is the Himalayan tahr. A pair of these animals, originally from the Himalayan mountains in northern India, escaped from the

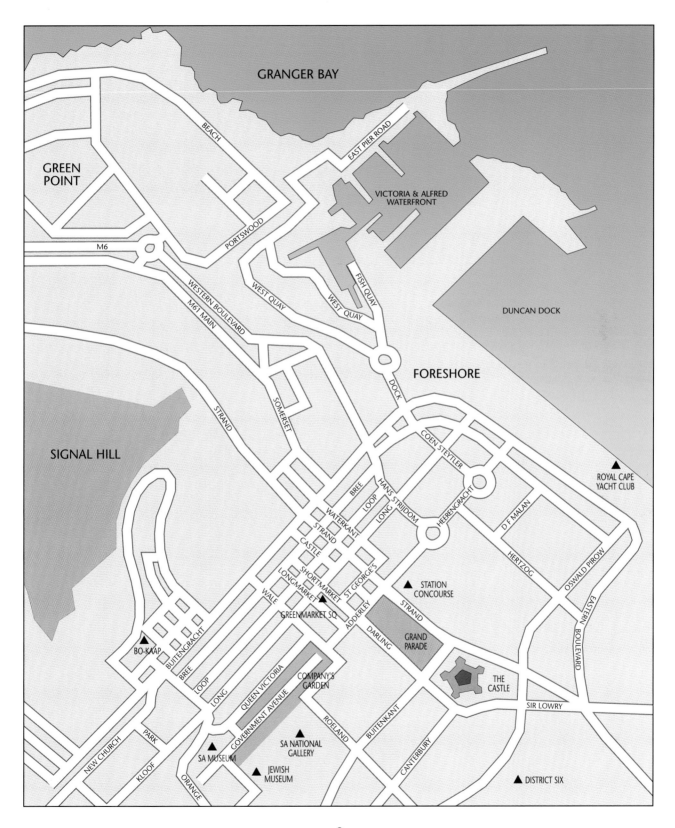

Groote Schuur Estate zoo in the 1930s and settled happily on Table Mountain. Unfortunately the tahrs cause a great deal of damage to local flora and their paths often lead to serious erosion. Regular culling programmes are organized, but there are still hundreds of these shy, goat-like animals living on the mountain.

The flora of the mountain is richly varied, with more than 500 species of erica and 100 species of iris. Botanists have long been fascinated by the incredibly wide variety of the Cape flora and estimate that more than 10 000 plant species are found here. They range from regal proteas to minute, ground-hugging ferns. Most of these occur on Table Mountain. The red disa, aptly dubbed the Pride of Table Mountain, grows in the cool, damp valleys in a number of places on the mountain and bears its flowers in January and February.

No visit to Cape Town is complete without a trip to the top of Table Mountain. All year round, queues of sightseers wait for their turn to travel in a swaying cable car on one of the most spectacular rides in the world. The view from the top, 1 067 metres above the sea, is breathtaking, whether one is looking over the city bowl and further to Table Bay or over the 'back' part of the mountain across the Twelve Apostles to the Atlantic ocean beyond Clifton and Camps Bay beaches.

The cableway is a two-car service that has been in operation for more than 60 years without a single accident. This is in part due to the interesting three-cable system by which it operates. The main cable carries the weight of the car, a thinner one pulls the cars along, and a third cable is there purely as a back-up; in fact, this cable has never been used. The two cars counter-balance each other, one making the upward journey while the other travels back down. The cableway operates on a daily basis weather permitting, and should the weather change for the worse, visitors are alerted to make their way back by means of a siren at the upper cable station.

There are hundreds of footpaths along the mountain's slopes and to the top for energetic hikers, as well as easy-to-follow rambles on the summit, marked with animal silhouettes. However, utmost care must be taken when walking – the benign-looking giant of Table Mountain has a nasty streak and has claimed the lives of several people during the past 10 years.

At the top of the mountain there is a souvenir shop, a post office where visitors can buy postcards and have them franked with a special Table Mountain postmark, and a rustic stone restaurant which serves light meals and refreshments. The summit is also a popular spot for picnics which are invariably interrupted by the fat, little rock rabbits – or dassies – some of which have become so tame that they will allow tourists to tickle them.

From the flat summit of Table Mountain the first-time visitor will get a better idea of the often confusing geography of this crooked finger of rock jutting into the stormy Atlantic Ocean, and of the layout of the city at its base. To the north and west is the vast expanse of ocean broken only by pin-point islands such as Gough and Tristan da Cunha between the Cape and South America.

Directly in front of the mountain is Table Bay with the notorious Robben Island in its centre. This little island has a sorry history of use as a jail for political prisoners, the most famous of whom was Nelson Mandela. Its future is undecided as the country heads into an age of change. Robben Island is populated by prison officials and their families, and although there are few prisoners there now, a high-security ferry still completes the voyage to and from the mainland every few hours.

The view of Table Mountain most often captured on postcards and popular paintings is the one from Bloubergstrand on the northern side of Table Bay. From here the three parts of Table Mountain – Lion's Head, 'the table', and Devil's Peak – can be most clearly seen.

Blouberg – or Blaauwberg in the original Dutch spelling – for many years consisted of just a handful of holiday shacks and fishermen's cottages dotted along the beachfront. It was a remote spot where anglers could be alone to cast their lines through pounding surf, or relax with a soothing bottle of good Cape wine and watch the sun set over the sea. Today, Blouberg is a fast-growing 'dormitory suburb' where rows of townhouses and large blocks of flats offering 'spectacular ocean views' are springing up like mushrooms.

To the south-east of the mountain is the wide expanse of level sandy land known as the Cape Flats. The greater part of this area is given over to low-income housing and industrial developments. Other, large parts of the Cape Flats are home to hundreds of thousands of black people who have been driven to the city from unproductive rural land in search of employment. They erect their make-shift homes from any material they can find, and so create the sprawling cities of plastic, wood and corrugated iron. These stand in sharp contrast to the more affluent 'white' suburbs of Cape Town with their gracious homes, shaded gardens, sports clubs and fine traditional schools.

From the stone restaurant at the top of the mountain, visitors look down on the pretty suburbs of Clifton and Camps Bay, where blocks of flats hug the seaside rocks and a series of sandy beaches provide sheltered swimming places. Further along to the south is the winding Marine Drive that takes travellers along the coast to Hout Bay past the row of buttress peaks known as the Twelve Apostles.

To make things easier for first-time visitors to the Cape, a detailed relief map has been set up on the mountain top, and this has helped thousands of people to unravel the puzzle of the Peninsula.

All too often, residents hear the familiar cry: 'I can't make head or tail of the Cape. The sea always seems to be on the wrong side.'

THE CITY BOWL

Cape Town's city centre is an intriguing mixture of old and new, formal and informal. Many of the fine ornate buildings from the 18th and 19th centuries, and older, have been preserved and restored to their former glory; splendid reminders of a less hurried age. These veterans stand

TOP: *With Table Mountain as a backdrop, the long, sandy beach at Blouberg provides a spectacular spot for a seaside picnic.*
ABOVE: *Bright, battened sails are set, ready to catch the breeze when these fast catamarans take to the surf at Blouberg.*

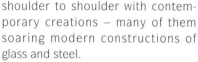

ABOVE: *Tuynhuys, presently the office of the State President.*
RIGHT: *The country's past is preserved in the Cultural History Museum.*

shoulder to shoulder with contemporary creations – many of them soaring modern constructions of glass and steel.

Complementing development on the ground is an extensive network of shopping malls below the city streets, connecting the railway station with the centre of the city. This underground labyrinth offers the opportunity to shop and browse without exposure to the weather, and provides easy access to ground level at several points.

For those who prefer the more traditional city, Long Street and Bree Street are particularly rich in old architecture, and the old civic buildings, such as the City Hall, the old Drill Hall, and the Cultural History Museum which is at the top end of Adderley Street, are fine examples of the styles of their times. The building housing the Cultural History Museum was erected in 1680 to accommodate 500 slaves for the Dutch East India Company. It later became the Supreme Court and then the Legislative Assembly building. The museum now contains a large collection of furniture, glassware, coins, weapons and other historic artifacts. The gable on the Parliament Street side bears an interesting detail by the early Cape sculptor, Anton Anreith. It

depicts a rather downcast lion being threatened by a unicorn, representing the Dutch supremacy over Britain. This is probably more out of wishful thinking than fact as the Dutch and British were almost continually at war at sea from 1680 for almost a century beyond.

Another historic hallmark of the city, and probably the oldest existing building in South Africa is the Castle. This fortress, which attracts thousands of visitors each year, was built in 1667 – replacing the original fortification made of earth – to protect the new settlement at the Cape from possible attack. The waves of Table Bay once lapped the walls of the Castle, but a massive reclamation programme, undertaken in the 1940s to dredge the bay, laid bare an area now known as the Foreshore. Today tall, modern office blocks, theatres, medical centres and hotels stand on land that was once the sea bed.

The Castle is designed in the form of a five-pointed star, each point named after a title held by Prince William of Orange; they are Katzenellenbogen, Buren, Nassau, Oranje and Leerdam. Extensive restoration of the Castle has been underway for several years and continues, one of the plans being to reconstruct the original moat and bridge. It now

incorporates a fascinating military museum reflecting much of the history of the Cape. Features of special interest are the graceful 'Kat' balcony designed by Anton Anreith, the main entrance gates housing a bell cast in Amsterdam in 1669, Lady Anne Barnard's ballroom, and the grim 'black hole' or dungeon where maximum security prisoners were housed in almost total darkness. Also on view is the William Fehr Art Collection named after the Cape businessman and art lover who travelled extensively overseas to retrieve items of Africana.

The city's main street, Adderley Street, links the foreshore area and harbour entrance to the historic 'Company's Garden', another great attraction in the city. A plaque at the entrance to the Gardens, as it is commonly known, tells of its origin: 'On April 29, 1652, the Company's gardener, Hendrick Boom, prepared the first piece of ground to carry into effect the instructions of the Lords Seventeen to Jan van Riebeeck to plant a vegetable garden and fruit garden at the Cape.' The harvest was to replenish the supplies of passing ships of the Dutch East India Company. Boom must have been a fine gardener, for it was only a few years later that Van Riebeeck recorded in his diary the harvesting of the first small crop of apples. Today the carefully tended botanic gardens contain exotic trees and shrubs from many countries: magnolias from Texas, plane trees from London, Puerto Rican hat palms, Australian firewheel trees and a holy peepul tree from India, to name but a few. They offer a peaceful refuge from the bustle of city life and act as the healthy lungs of the often polluted city.

A lane shaded by century-old oak trees, often frequented by squirrels, leads through the Gardens to the South African Museum, the South African National Gallery, and to the Jewish Museum which is housed in the oldest synagogue in South Africa.

The South African Museum, the oldest in the country, houses a fascinating collection of fossils of dinosaurs and other early inhabitants of Southern Africa, as well as a recently completed whale well, where visitors can see life-size models and complete skeletons of the whales that are found along the Cape coast. The museum contains several other informative natural history displays and a popular planetarium that offers varied programmes to budding astronomers.

The SA National Gallery contains a permanent collection of works by local and internationally known artists, many of which were donated by Sir Abe Bailey, the famous financier and politician who made his money on the Witwatersrand goldfields. Special exhibitons are held on a regular basis.

At the top end of the avenue another museum, Bertram House, dating back to 1839, contains an

RIGHT: *The newspaper seller's cry mingles with the myriad other sounds of the busy city.*
FAR RIGHT: *Summer music is made on every Cape Town street corner as buskers put a spring into a shopper's step.*

interesting collection of late Georgian and household treasures. It's a friendly little house that offers a very human glimpse of life at the Cape more than a century ago.

Also situated in the Gardens is Tuynhuys, now the office of South Africa's State President. The original building, erected in 1791, has been altered from time to time according to the dictates of the current head of state, and the resulting architecture reflects the whims of different political interest groups. The pediment is decorated with the insignia of the Dutch East India Company, a balcony bears the seal of William of Orange, and Lord Charles Somerset's ballroom was added during the days of colonial British rule. The British Empire also left its mark in the form of small crowns topping each lamp post along the avenue.

Situated alongside Tuynhuys are the Houses of Parliament, where so much of the country's turbulent history has been shaped and where the uncertain future of the land continues to be debated.

At the bottom end of the Gardens, Adderley Street continues naturally into Wale Street which in turn takes

one into an area known as the Bo-Kaap, or Upper Cape. This part of the city was once known as the 'Malay Quarter' and is home to many descendants of the Malay slaves brought to the Cape during the Dutch occupation in the 17th century. Most of its inhabitants are devout Muslims, and the sound of the mezzuin calling the faithful to prayer echoes through the streets five times each day here.

Many of the little houses in the Bo-Kaap have been restored, others have settled into a state of comfortable dilapidation. A small museum in Wale Street, the Bo-Kaap Museum, is devoted to the history of the Cape Malay people, and is well worth a visit, as is the authentic 'Biesmillah' restaurant.

Another prominent feature of the city centre, and very much part of the character here, are the colourful street markets. Cape Town has always echoed to the cries of street vendors: flower sellers in the alley between Adderley Street and Lower Plein Street, and fruit and vegetable vendors have long cried out with their monotonous shouts of 'four-for-a-rand peaches, four-for-a-rand'.

TOP: *Vendors set up their colourful stalls in Cape Town's St George's Mall open-air market.*
ABOVE: *Toy cyclists line up for sale in the Grand Parade, the Cape's oldest fleamarket.*

Probably the oldest existing street market in the country is the one on the Grand Parade in front of the old City Hall. For many decades vendors have displayed their wares here every Wednesday and Saturday, and it has become a treasure house of cut-price fabrics, inexpensive clothes and trinkets. A row of permanent fruit and vegetable stalls has been built and these operate all week long. Today the open-air market idea has spread to several parts of the city.

The newer street markets began with a few stalls in Greenmarket Square, originally the place where farmers brought their produce by wagon to sell to the town folk. Today there are leatherworkers, artists, African crafts, jewellery makers, booksellers and clothing stalls all over the square. Greenmarket Square proved such a success that other street markets have grown in the city: in St George's Mall, the station arcade, in Church Street and more informally in other spots too. The carnival atmosphere generated by these markets is enhanced by the sounds of street musicians, earning a good income by playing their drums, accordions, marimbas and saxophones; even tap-dancing to the beat of a 'ghetto-blaster' on the street corners.

THE WATERFRONT

Probably the most exciting attraction in modern Cape Town is the recently developed and very ambitious Victoria and Alfred Waterfront in the old harbour. (Yes, *Alfred* not *Albert*. Capetonians have grown accustomed to having to explain to visitors that the harbour is named after Queen Victoria and her son, Prince Alfred, who performed the official opening of the Alfred Basin while on a state visit to the colonies, and not after her beloved husband Albert.)

In line with the international trend to develop under-used waterfronts, the city recognized the opportunity to realize the potential of their own port. Together with a group of enterprising Cape Town businessmen they have turned large parts of the old harbour into a vibrant and cheerful tourist attraction that has captured the imaginations of visitors and Capetonians alike. The extent of the new development is breathtaking. Already there are restaurants, curio shops, museums, theatres, a brewery, pubs, a hotel, craft markets, a small amphitheatre and a busy shopping mall in an area which had become dilapidated and gloomy. Future plans make provision for an aquarium, a small craft harbour, exclusive seaside flats, more hotels and offices.

The real charm of the Waterfront is that all the development has been incorporated into a busy, working commercial harbour, where tugs hoot and fishing craft unload their catches. The building that houses the pump to empty the dry-dock has been converted into a busy pub, appropriately called The Pumphouse. During draining operations the pub thrums with the sound of the electric motor, causing drinks to rattle on the tables. On fine days visitors can sit outside The Pumphouse and watch the workers sandblasting rusty trawlers.

A fleet of pleasure boats takes sightseers on trips around the harbour and the old 'Penny Ferry' (alas no longer available for a penny) carries pub-crawlers from one waterside bar to another. Lazy Cape fur seals bask in the warm sun just metres away from sightseers and diners.

Like the open-air markets, the Waterfront has attracted a host of colourful entertainers who act, mime, sing, play and dance wherever they can gather an audience. With such a diversity of attractions on offer, it is small wonder that this venue became Cape Town's most popular tourist attraction during its very first year of operation. Parking within the Waterfront is plentiful, and for those who do not have their own cars a regular Waterfront bus service runs between it and the railway station in Adderley Street. More than any other urban development project, the Waterfront has injected new life into the Mother City. The mood here is vibrant and friendly and persists into the night, its visitors catered for by late-night shopping and ample entertainment.

THE ATLANTIC COAST

Leading away from the city centre and Waterfront activities is the road which skirts the Atlantic coast of the Cape Peninsula. The first part of this road winds through the high-rise flatlands of Green Point and Sea Point, but beyond these densely developed suburbs it emerges as one of the most spectacular routes in the world. Here, the road has been cut right into the mountainside, much of it hewn from solid rock (the surveyors who originally mapped the route often had to do so roped together like mountaineers).

Green Point and Sea Point are probably the most densely populated parts of the Peninsula. Here tall blocks of flats, both holiday and residential, stand shoulder to shoulder along many kilometres of sea front. But, an unexpected feature of almost every building, particularly in Sea Point, is a speciality restaurant at ground level devoted to a particular cuisine. Greek, Italian, Portuguese, French, Chinese and Japanese food is on offer. There are pavement cafés, fast-food outlets, steakhouses serving sizzling slabs of beef, pizza huts, seafood dens, chicken kitchens and ice-cream parlours. Whatever your culinary preference, Sea Point has it.

Sea Point, they say, never sleeps; its nightclubs and discos continue into the small hours, its restaurants cater for late-night diners and its pavements are always abuzz. It is vibrant, it's brash, it's noisy, but the residents love it and, so it would seem, do the rest of the Cape who come to share in the excitement when it is high-spirited entertainment that they require.

The Sea Point promenade, running for kilometres in front of Beach Road, is another lively meeting place. Sunset from here is often spectacular, but it is really only when you emerge from this busy built-up environment that the true beauty of the Atlantic coastline confronts you fully. After winding through the narrow streets of Bakoven, a suburb so small it often goes unnoticed, one embarks on an upward journey towards Clifton, a popular resort comprising four white-sanded beaches set well

ABOVE: *A worker in the V & A dry dock is dwarfed by the giant propeller of a ship undergoing repairs.*
RIGHT: *The airy shopping centre at the V & A Waterfront serves thousands of shoppers daily and stays open until late each night.*

below the level of the road. Clifton is surely one of the world's most idyllic settings and is famous for its shapely bikini-clad sun worshippers and prime cliffside bungalows.

Camps Bay, further along the coast, is a longer beach, fringed with tall palm trees and on a level with the road. It is popular with sunbathers and swimmers, although the water is usually chilly. The seafront is lined with restaurants, pavement cafés and smart hotels, all offering prime views of the clean white sand and turquoise ocean. It is also the setting of the popular Theatre on the Bay, where plays and musicals are performed all year round.

From here the coastal drive winds beneath the towering mountain buttresses known as the Twelve Apostles, offering panoramic vistas across the sea. Tucked away below

The rocky buttresses known as the Twelve Apostles tower above the Clifton and Camps Bay coastline.

the road is the hamlet of Llandudno, where smart seaside homes cling to the steep cliffsides and surround a well-protected, and yet another beautiful beach.

A pathway from the Llandudno car park leads to Sandy Bay, which has gained a reputation as the Cape's only (semi-official) nudist beach. Until quite recently this spot was regularly raided by police eager to stamp out 'public indecency' but the persecution has stopped and naturists can now soak up the sunshine to their hearts' content. Sandy Bay beach is totally undeveloped and provides no facilities, but it continues to attract its faithful devotees all year round.

The picturesque seaside village of Hout Bay lies beyond Llandudno. It is the home of a community of busy artists and crafts people, among others, whose independent spirit has prompted them to declare the area the 'Republic of Hout Bay'. This is only partly in jest. The once attractive fishing harbour of Hout Bay has now sadly declined into a rather untidy collection of concrete factory buildings. But there is Mariners' Wharf, a relatively new development offering a wide range of fresh fish, as well as delicious fish take-aways, a curio shop and a restaurant overlooking the bay. It is also worth taking the pleasure cruise round the bay to see the colony of seals frolicking on the surf-washed rocks of Duiker Island at the foot of the Sentinel Mountain.

Higher up the valley is another popular attraction: the World of Birds. Here visitors can stroll through airy aviaries of brightly plumed birds (more than 30 000) and examine them at close quarters. The aviary is much more than a tourist attraction though – it also acts as a sanctuary for injured birds which are brought in from all over the Peninsula.

Chapman's Peak Drive, leading out of Hout Bay to Noordhoek, is perhaps the Peninsula's most impressive route. Opened to traffic in 1922, it was carved out of the almost sheer rock face of the mountain, high above the surging surf. At its highest point there is a convenient parking area which affords a breathtaking view across Hout Bay to the Sentinel: a large buttress which seems to lean right over the sea. From this elevated lookout little boats leave their crisscross wakes on the bay while further out to sea the bigger oil tankers glide quietly past.

The road winds tortuously from the peak down to the rustic settlement of Noordhoek. Farms and smallholdings have been established for many years but many new residents have built homes here too, to take advantage of the rural atmosphere. The beach at Noordhoek, aptly named Long Beach and well-known as the surfing-championship venue, sweeps in a great wide arcing curve to Kommetjie, its unspoilt grandeur most striking as seen on the descent from Chapman's Peak. Kommetjie is one the few coastal spots in the Peninsula which has been spared intrusion from big developers. It offers a simple, uncomplicated existence away from (but still with easy reach of) the hurly-burly of the city. Kommetjie boasts a small hotel, a lighthouse and an attractive bathing pool, set amid a few streets of modest but attractive houses.

The countryside beyond Kommetjie becomes wilder and is practically uninhabited. The road winds past the tiny settlements of Soetwater and Scarborough whose landmark is a rock carved by the wind into the shape of a camel. The coastline here is wild and rough all the way to Cape Point, the tip of the Peninsula and the western edge of False Bay.

THE FALSE BAY COAST

To the south and east of the Cape Peninsula is the great sweep of sea called False Bay. It begins at Cape Point, the most southerly point of the Peninsula, and ends at a mountain peak called Cape Hangklip (hanging rock) which towers above the sea. Along the coastline between the two points is a fascinating patchwork of quaint villages, beaches and holiday resorts. Some of the beaches are diminutive, some sheltered, even hidden by rocks and dense bush. Others consist of large, unbroken expanses of sand. There are promenades, coastal walks, a charming collection of shops, a fishing harbour and naval base; and the added attraction of whales, which visit the bay every spring.

The whales arrive in False Bay in about August each year and are greeted with great delight by visitors

and residents. These southern right whales come into the sheltered waters of the bay to give birth, and to court and mate. Often they move close inshore, swimming just metres from the rocks, parallel to the coastline, and at night their soft, booming blowing can be heard from several hundred metres away. The sight of these slow-moving giants of the ocean, passing along on their silent and mysterious business and occasionally sending up a plume of misty spray, is a real privilege.

The southern tip of the Cape Peninsula has been turned into an attractive 800-hectare reserve, the Cape of Good Hope Nature Reserve, which contains a wealth of interesting

flora and fauna. There are eight species of buck, ostriches, baboons and tortoises, as well as many smaller creatures. Of particular interest are the baboons within the reserve which are unique in that they have adapted to an inter-tidal shore life, finding food among the rock pools at low tide. Baboons may also be encountered outside of the reserve alongside the road. These animals provide hours of entertainment as they scamper on to the roofs and bonnets of parked cars. But feeding them is strictly prohibited as it establishes a dependency which may lead to aggressive behaviour.

Within the reserve plant- and bird-life is also varied and plentiful, and to get the fullest enjoyment from this natural beauty spot one should drive slowly and stop along the little side roads wherever possible. Better still, enjoy a walk on one of the many hiking paths. The reserve deserves a full day's visit, but all too often it is included as a quick stopping place in a rushed day-trip round the whole Peninsula. Situated on an impressive pinnacle of rock at the very tip of the

TOP: *Camps Bay beach is a favourite spot for sun worshippers.*
LEFT: *A launch loaded with day trippers circles Hout Bay below the cliffs of Chapman's Peak.*

TOP: *Catching the big one at the Hoek, a surfer begins his exhilarating ride to the shore.*
ABOVE: *This restored cottage is typical of an earlier style of rural homestead at the Cape.*

Peninsula is the original Cape Point lighthouse – a sight worth making the fairly steep walk from the parking area for. The less energetic can cadge a ride on the *Flying Dutchman* bus which takes passengers to the top. This lighthouse is no longer in use because at this lofty height it is often obscured from the lookouts of passing ships by low-lying sea mist. A new lighthouse has therefore been erected some way down the face of the cliff. It has one of the most powerful lights in the world and has saved many ships from destruction on this rocky 'Cape of Storms'. From the pinnacle one can look back along the spine of the Peninsula, which lies in the sea like a great sleeping dragon, all the way to Table Mountain. On the right is the curving sweep of False Bay, about 40 km across, and to the left is the endless blue of the Atlantic. There are several pleasant beaches in the reserve, as well as picnic areas, fishing spots and a restaurant in an old farmhouse. Venus Pool offers safe bathing in a natural rock pool, while Platboom is a ideal for a picnic. The reserve is also a favourite spot from which to launch a ski-boat for a day's fishing off the point.

From the entrance to the Cape of Good Hope Nature Reserve the False Bay road passes high above the sheltered, but almost inaccessible, Smitswinkel Bay where determined holiday-makers have built a cluster of wooden houses. There is no access at all to vehicles and all tools and building materials were carried down the steep cliffside by hand. In recent years the stripped hulks of several redundant ships – some formerly of the South African Navy – have been sunk in the deep part of Smitswinkel Bay to form artificial reefs in the hope of attracting sea life. Divers report that this area is now teeming with marine creatures.

Miller's Point, further along this scenic drive, is the launching spot for many ski-boats; weekend parking is always a problem here because of all the boat trailers. A tidal pool attracts bathers, and nearby there is The Black Marlin, an excellent seafood restaurant which has one of the best wine-lists in the Cape.

Boulders is a beautiful little beach just outside Simon's Town. It is also home to a thriving colony of jackass penguins which have become completely unafraid of humans, and are seen to frolic in the sea alongside bathers. Boulders is one of the most sheltered of the Cape beaches, but has become so popular (possibly because of its penguin residents) that it has been turned into a pay beach to limit numbers. It's a great favourite for family groups, but in the summer season it is best to arrive early as the gates are closed when the beach reaches its capacity.

The pretty maritime village of Simon's Town is a place of great charm and historical interest, and home of the South African Navy. Sailors in smart white naval uniforms add a special character to the town, and a thriving shopping centre offers shoppers surprising bargains in clothing and electronic goods – often at prices far below those charged by the large shopping chains. There's an interesting craft centre, several good restaurants and tearooms, and a town square where craft markets are held at weekends. The square overlooks the Simon's Town yacht basin, which provides a busy but attractive background for those shopping or enjoying tea under the spreading eucalyptus tree.

The statue erected in the square has a heart-warming tale behind it. This unusual memorial is to the Royal Naval dog, Just Nuisance, who befriended hundreds of lonely sailors far from home during World War II and became a legend during his lifetime. Just Nuisance was known to take charge of sailors who had had too much to drink, to guide them to the Simon's Town train and lead them back to their barracks. Time has probably added a good deal of detail to some of the stories about this extraordinary dog, but it remains a popular local legend and generates quite a good trade in Just Nuisance memorabilia, from T-shirts to coffee mugs. There's a special Just Nuisance display in the Simon's

Town Museum, where tourists can follow the life story of this remarkable canine matelot.

From Simon's Town the road winds past the little hamlet of Glencairn with its cosy seaside pub, to Fish Hoek, South Africa's only 'dry' town where no liquor may be sold. This rule was instituted many years ago when wagons, taking supplies to the sailing ships anchored in Simon's Bay from Cape Town, used to spend the night in Fish Hoek Bay. Local residents wanting to earn a few extra pounds would ply the wagoners with drink. They often ended up in such a poor condition that they were unable to control their teams of oxen the following day; several wagons were lost down the steep mountain slopes along the way. When the land was eventually granted to a farmer, Jan Bruyns, it was given on the strict condition that no alcohol be sold on it. The regulation has remained in force in spite of frequent attempts to have it changed. Every effort to bring about a change is stoutly opposed by traditionalists, who have even formed an association known as the 'Defenders of Fish Hoek'. So far, they

TOP: *Famous canine matelot, Just Nuisance, stares out across False Bay from Simon's Town's Jubilee Square.*
MIDDLE: *The great rocks at Boulders beach provide shelter and privacy.*
RIGHT: *Simon's Town shops display their bright wares.*

Diners and drinkers can sit in comfort overlooking the breakers crashing just a few metres below them. There is a variety of bric-a-brac and antique shops along the Main Road in Kalk Bay which can often reward an hour of rummaging.

St James, a small resort further along the road, became sought after when it was realized that the area was largely sheltered from the gale-force south-easters that batter the rest of this coastline in summer. This is probably why it was chosen for the holiday homes of Cecil John Rhodes and Sir Abe Bailey whose houses can still be seen here. Rhodes' Cottage has been converted into an interesting little museum devoted to the history of this famous pioneer. A safe tidal pool at St James beach attracts hundreds of sun-worshipping families every summer weekend.

At Muizenberg the coastline turns eastwards, forming a pleasant bay for surfers and bathers. It is one of the largest and most popular beaches on the Peninsula. Brightly painted wooden changing booths line the beach, adding to the holiday atmosphere. The beach front at Muizenberg is an ideal spot for children, with attractions ranging from miniature golf to a water slide. Sadly, the village area has deteriorated over the years and many of the once gracious houses have been converted into weather-beaten blocks of flats. There is much talk of rejuvenating the area, but progress so far is painfully slow.

Just inland from Muizenberg is Marina da Gama, an attractive housing development built on the banks of artificially dredged canals alongside a natural lagoon. Clusters of white-walled houses flank the waterside and lawns roll down to the canal edges. Small craft are moored at jetties and residents sail or row to neighbours nearby. The waterside development won several architectural awards and has provided a lifestyle unusual for South Africans.

ABOVE: *The tidal pool in St James is a popular swimming place.*
OPPOSITE: *The waterfront homes at Marina da Gama provide residents with a gracious and relaxed lifestyle.*
OPPOSITE RIGHT: *With its channels, bays and islands, Marina da Gama is one of the country's most successful marina developments.*

have triumphed in all their battles against the sale of the demon alcohol in their village.

Along the coast is another quaint seaside village, Kalk Bay, home of hundreds of fishermen who carry out their trade in sturdy little boats, using hand-lines to catch that Cape delicacy, snoek. Kalk Bay also has a popular restaurant, the Brass Bell, located right on the railway platform.

From Muizenberg the False Bay coast curves in a great arc of golden sand, largely undeveloped and unused, except by a few regular fishermen and bathers who like to be away from the crowds. The coast road, Baden-Powell Drive, is a popular route for Sunday drives and passes spectacular white cliffs where thousands of black-backed gulls have nests in a fenced-in gull sanctuary.

On the opposite side of the bay from Fish Hoek coast are the holiday resorts of Strand and Gordon's Bay, both favourite launching spots for boat fishermen. Although the fish population has been seriously depleted by commercial fishermen over the years, False Bay is still a popular area for ski-boat anglers and fishermen casting into the breakers from the beach.

The bay is also home to a huge population of Cape fur seals which, fishermen claim, have enjoyed more than their fair share of the fish, and is reputed to contain a fair number of great white sharks too, attracted to the bay by the seal population. Fortunately the sharks appear to prefer the taste of seals and no attacks on bathers have been reported for many years. Shark-hunting has now been banned in order to preserve the shark population – and to ensure that the seal population in the bay does not become too large!

A form of fishing peculiar to False Bay is 'trek fishing', which is carried on in its traditional form. Small, sturdy rowing boats are taken out through the surf and rowed in a wide circle, while the fisherman in the stern of the boat pays out a long, narrow net. Once the circle of net has been deployed the boat returns to the beach and all hands – from holiday-makers to local residents – are summoned to pull in the net line. Sometimes the catch consist of little more than a few, small fish, but there are times when a rich haul of yellowtail is brought ashore and all who lent a hand are rewarded with fish to take home. This form of fishing will in all probability vanish into history within the next few decades, and will linger only in faded photographs, along with those of the whaling craft that once plied the bay.

Most Capetonians refer to the False Bay side of the Peninsula as the 'Indian Ocean' side, although this is not entirely accurate. Officially, the Atlantic and Indian oceans meet at Cape Agulhas, the southernmost tip of Africa. This puts both sides of the Cape Peninsula firmly in the Atlantic.

In reality, however, the warm Agulhas Current that sweeps southward along the Indian Ocean side of Africa meets the cooler Benguela Current of the Atlantic at Cape Point – the southern tip of the Cape Peninsula – so there seems good reason to claim Cape Point as the true meeting place of the two oceans. This, however, does not account for the warmer waters (by several degrees) of the False Bay beaches compared to those at Clifton or Sea Point on the other side of the Peninsula. This phenomenon is as a result of the prevailing summer south-east wind which blows the warmer upper layer of water towards the False Bay beaches while sweeping that warm layer away on the Clifton side, leaving the icy water to well up from the depths of the ocean.

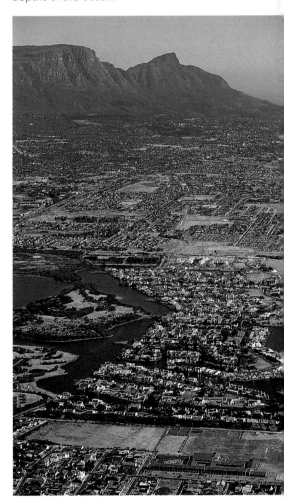

History in Stone

As can be expected from South Africa's oldest settlement, the Cape abounds in places of historical interest. The people of the Cape have a deep sense of history and many of the old buildings and sites have been carefully preserved and restored.

Situated in the Constantia valley is one of the best-known examples of Cape Dutch homes:

Groot Constantia is the oldest surviving farmstead in the Cape set within the grounds of the well-known wine estate. Originally built by Governor Simon van der Stel who lived there until he died, it was taken over in 1778 by Hendrick Cloete who was responsible for developing the legendary sweet Constantia wines: it is said that Napoleon called for a glass of Constantia wine on his deathbed on St Helena. This gracious estate is open to the public all year round. It includes two restaurants and a wine museum. The manor house is also a museum, filled with furniture, paintings and domestic items of historic interest. The well-equipped kitchen offers a good idea of the lifestyle of the early Cape settlers, while the slave quarters below the house show another facet of life in those times.

The Groote Schuur Estate on the eastern slopes of Table Mountain also contains some fine examples of Cape architecture:

Groote Schuur means 'big barn' and was originally used as a granary in the 17th century. The barn was later converted to a house, which burned down in 1896 and was rebuilt by Sir Herbert Baker to become the Cape Town home of Cecil John Rhodes. Rhodes bequeathed it, and its surrounding estates, to the nation, and the house now serves as the official residence of the State President.

Rhodes Memorial, on the upper slopes of Groote Schuur Estate, is an imposing memorial to the great Empire Builder. It consists of a stone classical temple (made from granite quarried from Table Mountain), a huge bronze equestrian statue of Physical Energy and two rows of bronze lions. There's a tearoom and deer park there and at night the site offers a spectacular view across the lighted city. It is traditionally a favourite meeting place for lovers.

University of Cape Town Also on the original Groote Schuur Estate is the beautiful University of Cape Town, one of South Africa's bastions of academic freedom and for many years the country's only medical school. Its teaching hospital, Groote Schuur, became internationally famous in 1967 when Professor Chris Barnard performed the world's first heart transplant operation there. The university is deeply involved in many research projects ranging from studies of the ocean currents and marine life to the acoustic properties of materials used in car manufacturing. The campus has expanded steadily to cope with increasing numbers of students, and one of the interesting old buildings now incorporated in the Lower Campus is the The Woolsack, an attractive house (also Baker designed) and once used as a summer home by author Rudyard Kipling. Several of Kipling's *Just So Stories* for children were written here. Today The Woolsack is a student residence.

Mostert's Mill, just below the main university campus, is the only Dutch windmill in the Cape still in working order. The original owner and miller, Sybrand Mostert, farmed on the site and erected the mill in 1796. The mill is open to the public, and there is a group of keen historians who hope to put it back into service. A similar project has been undertaken

TOP: *The gracious Groote Schuur, designed by Herbert Baker.*
LEFT: *Set in the oak-shaded Constantia valley, Buitenverwachting combines traditional architecture with modern technology.*

in Newlands where an old water-driven mill, The Josephine Mill, now produces stone-ground flour and is open to visitors as a milling museum.

KIRSTENBOSCH

The tiny enclave of the southern and western Cape is one of the world's richest botanic regions – in fact, one of its six floral kingdoms. In spite of its small area (the region constitutes only 0,04 per cent of the world's surface) it contains more than 8 500 indigenous plant species, including some so rare that they occur in areas only a few square metres in extent. The immense wealth of the plant life here has attracted botanists since before the first European settlement, and even today botanists travel from all over the world to Cape Town to study the floral treasure.

In many great cities the indigenous flora has been swallowed up by urban sprawl. Cape Town, however, is fortunate to have one of the world's leading botanic gardens right in its midst. Kirstenbosch, headquarters of the

National Botanical Institute of South Africa, has a spectacular setting on the eastern slopes of Table Mountain and was established in 1913 on land bequeathed to the nation by Cecil John Rhodes. It covers an area of more than 500 hectares, of which 36 hectares are cultivated. The rest of the area consists of a natural flora reserve. This spot happens to have one of the highest rainfalls in South Africa, with an average of some 1 400 mm being registered annually.

Presently more than 6 000 indigenous plant species are cultivated at Kirstenbosch, and visitors can enjoy this rich diversity as they stroll along the winding pathways. Attractions include many varieties of proteas, ericas, cycads, pelargoniums and ferns. For those with the patience to look for them, some of the most charming flowers are the tiny ones that hug the earth beneath their more eye-catching neighbours. Near the boundary of the garden fragments of the original hedge of wild almonds, planted in 1660 by Jan van Riebeeck to protect the

TOP LEFT: *At Kirstenbosch Botanical Gardens natural beauty and serious research combine.* **RIGHT:** *The protea, queen of the Cape's indigenous flowers, comes in a wide variety of shapes and colours. Two members of the famous family are* Mimetes hirtus *(above) and* Protea aristata *(below).*

settlers' cattle and sheep, can still be seen. The remaining parts of this hedge in Kirstenbosch and on Wynberg Hill have been proclaimed a National Monument.

The shaded paths of Newlands forest are a favourite spot for city walkers and their dogs.

Knowledgeable guides are available to conduct groups around the gardens, and the blind are catered for on the Braille Trail and in the scented garden where aromatic plants encourage visitors to use their senses of touch and smell. Behind the large, beautifully tended gardens there is much else happening. Important botanic research is carried out in the Compton Herbarium at the gardens, and there are well-used exhibition and lecture facilities, as well as a fine tearoom and souvenir shop. Once a year the gardens hold sales of indigenous plants, and gardeners from all over the Peninsula come to stock up. Hugely popular in summer is the sunset concerts hosted by the gardens on Sunday evenings when all manner of musicians entertain the crowds as they picnic on the lawns.

Today Kirstenbosch is a haven of peace where many come to escape the rush of city life and re-establish contact with nature. For some it's a brisk hour's walk along one of the many hiking routes, for others it offers a shady spot in which to enjoy a good book. Even for those with no interest at all in plants, it's an enchanting place to be. The renowned naturalist William Burchell so accurately described the area when he wrote: '... the most picturesque of any I have seen in the vicinity'.

NATURE WALKS

The Cape's mild weather and spectacular scenery makes it ideal for walkers and hikers. The choice of routes is almost endless and even those who have lived here all their lives still discover new and exciting places for a weekend ramble.

The Silvermine Nature Reserve, reached via the Ou Kaapseweg (Old Cape Road), is a popular picnic spot, with facilities for braaiing under the shady pine trees. There are also several scenic walks within the reserve, most of which offer hikers breathtaking views down over False Bay and the Cape Flats, and even over to Hout Bay in the distance.

Another favourite spot for a pleasant weekend ramble is the Newlands Forest just above Union Avenue in Newlands. There's plenty of parking space alongside the road, and the forest is further criss-crossed by meandering footpaths and pretty streams. Further along the mountain slope the Cecilia Forest plantation offers another attractive woodland walk, which can be reached from the parking area near the popular Constantia Nek restaurant.

THE PEOPLE

In every busy seaport around the world you'll find people of all nations gathered. The ocean is their workplace and they are drawn together by a common love and respect for the sea. And always, if the place is hospitable and the climate good, some of them leave the sea and settle ashore. It is no surprise, therefore, that a beautiful city like Cape Town should have a cosmopolitan population. It is as if all the nations of the world have been tossed into a pot and stirred well to create the People of the Cape: an interesting, often colourful collection of occupants with quite distinct origins.

Long before the first daring Portuguese explorer, Bartholomew Diaz, rounded the Cape in 1488 with a leaky ship and a crew close to mutiny, the small yellow San people already knew the Peninsula as a good hunting ground and a source of food and water. In 1652 the Dutch East India Company established a victualling station for ships, and traded with these indigenous people. And then sailors arrived from Portugal, Holland, Britain and France. Many fell in love with this rocky outcrop; some stayed behind.

The hard-working Dutch settlers established agriculture and developed the infrastructure of the budding settlement – reservoirs, water-courses, roads, fortifications. Many of their well-built structures survive today. They left a style of gabled, white-washed architecture that today is distinctively Cape and can be seen on many of the older farmsteads and gracious homes. The Dutch also laid the foundation of a new language, Afrikaans.

These early settlers imported slaves from their colonies in the Far East, and the descendants of those slaves, the Cape Malay people, developed their own customs and lifestyle that are still alive today.

Their distinctive style of highly spiced dishes has become part of the Cape's culinary tradition.

And then there were the French: the Huguenots, fleeing from religious persecution in Europe in 1688, found a safe haven at the Cape and brought with them traditions of gracious living, appreciation of the arts, fine food and wine. Many of them settled in the beautiful and fertile Franschhoek valley, where the wine farms bear French names like La Motte, L'Ormarins, La Provence and L'Arc d'Orléans to this day. Although this small French group was quickly absorbed into the Dutch community, their influence lives on in many of the common Afrikaans surnames such as Du Preez, Marais, De Villiers, Malan and Le Roux, to mention a few.

The British people also had a marked effect on life at the Cape. They added their formality and love of good order, and set up systems of justice, military defence and government. The families of the ruling colonial aristocracy tended to stay aloof from the common people, but their influence is still strongly evident in the stately homes of Bishopscourt and Constantia, the architecture of Sir Herbert Baker, and the imprint left by those two most enthusiastic empire builders, Cecil John Rhodes and his life-long friend, Rudyard Kipling. The British tradition lives, too, in the fine old schools like Diocesan College, St Cyprians and SACS, all run very much along traditional public school lines.

Many thousands of Jewish families, fleeing from persecution in eastern Europe during the Czarist pogroms in Russia and Poland, and later from the Nazi holocaust in Germany, arrived in the Cape. Friendless and destitute, they established businesses which, through sheer hard work and determination, thrived and grew into many of today's household-name chain stores.

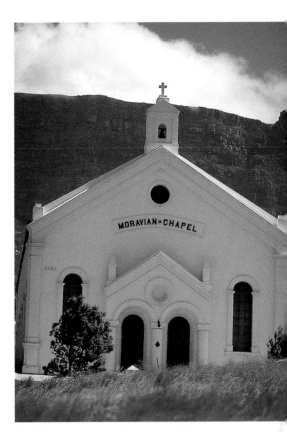

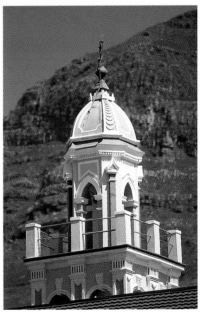

TOP AND ABOVE: *Once in the heart of a thriving congregation, the Moravian Chapel in District Six now stands in lonely isolation. From the mosque tower nearby, the faithful are still called to prayer.*

And from within the country itself, the Xhosa people of the eastern Cape who came seeking employment, settled down to their own style of urban living. While retaining strong ties with their origins, they have adopted a zestful, American-jazz style of life which characterizes the townships. Xhosa families continue to arrive in the Cape in their thousands, driven from their homes and farms by drought and lack of work. Their makeshift houses form the vast sprawling settlements of Crossroads and Khayelitsha (meaning 'The New Home') on the Cape Flats. Many other black people live in the more structured suburbs of Guguletu, Langa and Nyanga.

The indomitable humour of the so-called 'coloured' folk – people of mixed ancestry – has an earthy, bantering style of its own. The sharp repartee usually heard in fishing harbours, markets and commuter trains provides non-stop entertainment for those with the ear to hear it.

Add to this the sailors and whalermen from Scandinavia, China, Japan and Korea, and the mixture gathers richness. These are the people of the western Cape.

This interesting blend of Cape characters includes the delightfully philosophical 'bergies': people of the mountain. They have earned their name because for many years they lived in caves on the slopes of Table Mountain, descending to the city to scratch out a living during the day and returning to their mountain lairs at night. Modern 'bergies' are more likely to sleep in railway subways, shopping malls or any other spots sheltered from the elements. They are known for their cheeky humour and calm disregard for authority. Many earn a living by collecting bottles, paper and cardboard for sale to recyclers.

At the other end of the social scale are the wealthy elite of suburbs such as Bishopscourt, Newlands and Constantia, where weekends are for bridge, tennis and swimming.

The population is mixed and varied, and there are obviously tensions and differences, but the people of

Farm workers near Paarl harvest the succulent 'waterblommetjies' that form the basis for a traditional and delicious stew.

Cape Town are, on the whole, just a little more relaxed and friendly than those in most other South African cities. It would seem that the Mediterranean climate of this tiny corner of the country soaks into the very bones of the people here.

History leaves its scars, and we cannot simply gloss over the effects that more than 40 years of apartheid rule have had on the people of the Cape. Neighbourhoods were arbitrarily declared 'white' areas and families were moved away – often forcefully – to alternate areas. The sprawling, noisy, racially mixed neighbourhood known as District Six to the east of the city centre was cleared, buildings were bulldozed to the ground and the people sent to new homes on the Cape Flats among neighbours they did not know. What was once a vibrant district of tailors, craftsmen, fishmongers, fruit vendors and shop-keepers is now a wasteland; it's future is still undecided.

In the wealthy 'white' suburb of Newlands is St Andrew's Church, once the spiritual home of many 'coloured' families living there. They were moved out to make way for white families, but the church officers and congregation still travel to New-lands – often many kilometres – every Sunday to worship at their old church. The same happened to Muslim families living in Simon's Town. They were forced to move to the new settlement of Ocean View, near Kommetjie, but the little mosque in the naval town is still their religious home.

Wherever communities are broken apart and strangers are thrown together arbitrarily, social standards decline and crime increases. The Cape Peninsula owes its high crime rate largely to the cruel disruptions of the apartheid era.

This policy has undoubtedly disrupted the normal development of the people of South Africa. Perhaps the Cape, with its natural spirit of tolerance and warmth, will be the first of the country's communities to heal the wounds of apartheid. Unfortunately, the scars will be there for many more years.

THE WEATHER

To the south of South Africa the ocean takes the form of an unbroken circle of water extending right around the globe. This is the only place on Earth where this occurs, and the result is a series of interesting weather patterns at different times of the year.

In this Southern Ocean the winds generated by the spin of the Earth are unhindered by any land masses and can build up tremendous force and speed. This is the region of the notorious Roaring Forties so feared by mariners throughout history, and is the reason why the Cape earned itself the title of 'Cape of Storms': there are literally hundreds of known shipwrecks all along the coast testifying to this name.

In winter, when the Earth's pressure and wind belts move northwards, the frontal systems travelling up from the cold polar regions impinge directly on the weather at the Cape. These cold fronts bring cold northerly winds and persistent rain. The western Cape is thus often gloomy and wet in winter while the rest of the country experiences very dry winters with, for the most part, mild sunny days. Cape Town residents are philosophical about their weather, however. The Cape is at its greenest during winter, they say, and the gentle sunny days between the cold fronts are without doubt the best days of the year. At these times the air is washed clean and the green countryside sparkles in the champagne light; the days of cold and damp are quickly forgotten and smiles beam out over the Peninsula.

During the summer months most of the fronts pass harmlessly to the south, and all the Cape experiences is the strong south-east wind that often reaches gale force, particularly over False Bay. When the summer south-easter blows, Table Mountain is covered by a white mantle of cloud known, rather obviously, as the 'tablecloth'.

The Cape south-easter is not all bad, by any means. Local residents call it the Cape Doctor, as it blows away much of the accumulated air pollution and cools the city which, because of its setting in the sheltered crook of the mountain's arm, would otherwise be unbearably hot. Summers are therefore very pleasant; it is rarely too hot and the absence of any significant rainfall makes for predictable, fine days.

The high rocky spine sprawled right across the Peninsula is also responsible for some interesting weather happenings in Cape Town. Very often it is pleasantly calm and sunny on one side of the Peninsula while the other side, only a few kilometres away, is experiencing heavy rain or very windy conditions. This is because the steep slopes of the mountain act as barriers, deflecting clouds and moist winds away from areas on the other side. So, before you abandon a picnic planned for a particular beach, check the weather on the other side first.

Canoeing is a popular pastime in the Cape. Here a lone paddler puts in some training for one of the long river races.

ABOVE: *The academic town of Stellenbosch is rich in fine old buildings like the Victoria College, inaugurated in 1886, and also known as the Ou Hoofgebou.*
OPPOSITE: *Gracious restored Cape Dutch homesteads, like this one at Neethlingshof, are part of the Stellenbosch Wine Route.*

The mountain chain is also the reason for the high rainfall in Newlands, South Africa's wettest suburb, which nestles on the eastern slopes of Table Mountain. When the moisture-laden north-westerly wind reaches the Cape, it is swept upward by the mountain slopes behind Clifton and Sea Point. As it rises, the temperature drops sharply and the moisture condenses as rain – directly above Newlands. This rainfall supplements the frontal rain already falling throughout Cape Town in winter, to make Newland's rainfall average much higher than other parts of the city.

WINELANDS OF THE CAPE

After establishing a settlement at the Cape, one of the very first things that Dutch pioneer Jan van Riebeeck did was to import vine cuttings and plant vineyards for the production of wine. In 1655, just three years after landing at the Cape, Van Riebeeck received his first shipment of vines from Europe and planted them in the Company's Garden. Four years later, on 2 February 1659, he wrote joyfully in his diary: 'Today, praise to the Lord, wine was made for the first time from Cape grapes'.

He was so encouraged by this achievement that he planted a further 1 000 vines on the slopes of the mountain and called the spot Wynberg, the Wine Mountain. The great wine-making tradition of the Cape had begun. Today more than 3 000 different wines are produced in the Cape, each with its distinctive style and character. Van Riebeeck's successor, Simon van der Stel,

expanded the budding wine industry dramatically by planting a hundred thousand vines on his farm, Groot Constantia. Today, more than three centuries later, Van der Stel's farm is still one of the most beautiful in the Cape and the wines of Groot Constantia are enjoyed by wine-lovers from all over the world.

The Groot Constantia Estate is one of three estates which combine to form the Constantia Wine Route set within the heart of suburban Cape Town. The other two well-known wine farms are Klein Constantia and Buitenverwachting, the latter also with a restaurant serving superlative fare. All three of these historic cellars produce excellent award-winning wines, and although modernized, have succeeded in retaining an aura of antiquity. The high-tech cellars at Klein Constantia are particularly impressive and have won design awards for the best concrete constructions of their kind in South Africa. A speciality of this historic wine area is the wine made from Sauvignon Blanc grapes, which seem to do particularly well here.

For many visitors to the Cape, a holiday is incomplete without a trip into the beautiful winelands of Stellenbosch and Paarl. The best known of the wine routes is that of Stellenbosch. Established more than 20 years ago it has grown from a handful of tentative pioneers to a whole district of fascinating farms and co-operative cellars, all open to the public for tastings and sales, many offering cellar tours, light meals and other wine-related entertainment. The wines of the Stellenbosch area vary widely in style, from noble oak-matured reds to frivolous young white wines and sweet fortified ports and jerepigoes.

A visit to the university town of Stellenbosch offers far more than just wine, however. It is a voyage back into history. The old town has been beautifully restored and in the oak-shaded Dorp Street almost every building bears the bronze plaque of the National Monuments Commission. The Stellenbosch Village Museum, a fine collection of historic buildings, offers an intimate look at life from 1709 to 1877. Stellenbosch has a proud tradition of providing good hospitality, and there is a wealth of excellent restaurants and wine houses in the town.

The Paarl wine route is a little further afield than that of Stellenbosch but is still within comfortable reach of Cape Town. This area also produces a wide range of wines and is the headquarters of the Koöperatiewe Wijnbouwersvereniging or KWV, controlling body of the Cape wine industry. Nederburg, probably the best-known wine label in the country, is also located in Paarl and the annual Nederburg auction of rare wines is one of the highlights of the Cape wine calendar.

Nestling at the foot of the Groot Drakenstein mountains, Franschhoek has some of the finest restaurants in South Africa, including the award-winning Le Quartier Français, and La Petite Ferme overlooking the scenic Franschhoek valley. The town was established by French Huguenots who fled from religious persecution in 1688, bringing their traditions of elegant culture with them.

An imposing monument to those French pioneers forms the focal point of the village. The wine farms in the area specialize in wines that are crisp, elegant and high in fruity acids. Many visitors return home with glowing memories of a gracious lunch under the tall oaks at nearby Boschendal, one of the Cape's best-known wine estates, matching fine cuisine with equally fine wines.

There are other less popularized, but highly recommended wine routes in the Cape region, notably those of the West Coast and of Robertson. Both of these areas are further from Cape Town, and perhaps too distant to tackle in a day's outing.

In fact visitors need not travel at all in order to enjoy the wines. The Peninsula abounds in good specialist wine shops where most of the Cape's wines can be found. Some, such as the Vaughan Johnson Wine Shop on the Waterfront, have tasting facilities allowing you to taste before you buy. Cape restaurants, too, are becoming increasingly aware of the importance of serving fine wines with their food and the quality of their wine lists is improving at a rapid rate.

ABOVE: *The old Houw Hoek Inn, once a stage coach stopping place, is now a peaceful weekend getaway.*

LEFT: *Delicate watsonias form part of the Cape's rich floral heritage.*

SCENIC DRIVES FROM CAPE TOWN

The Cape Peninsula is surrounded by a variety of interesting places to visit, all within just an hour or two's drive by car or bus.

One of the most attractive routes in the country is the drive along the coast from Gordon's Bay to Hermanus. This road takes travellers around Cape Hangklip, past a host of small settlements of mostly weekend cottages at Kogel Bay, Rooiels and Pringle Bay. There is a wilder sort of beauty here, quite different from the lush greenery of the Peninsula, and by comparison quite bleak. Here the vegetation thins and the rugged mountain area takes on a forbidding nature. Great tumbled piles of bare rock form the habitat of roving troops of baboons and occasional mountain leopards.

Further along the coast is the popular resort of Kleinmond, and further again, Hermanus (about 120 km from Cape Town), a fashionable and beautiful getaway where the more affluent residents of Cape Town have holiday homes. Hermanus is a prime whale-viewing site in spring when these gentle giants move into the bay to calve. The town has even appointed an official Whale Crier, who announces the day's best whale-viewing spots and heralds the arrival of the great mammals by blowing his kelp horn. There is a selection of excellent restaurants and hotels, some scenic mountain drives, hiking routes in the Fernkloof Nature Reserve and a large lagoon with various water craft.

Once the centre of a thriving fishing industry, Hermanus has a good fishing museum at the old harbour and some of its small craft have been preserved. A spectacular coastal walk has been created along the clifftop at Hermanus, taking ramblers past steep cliffs and narrow inlets where the sea roars and thunders against the rocks below. When visiting this attractive town, it's well worth spending an hour or two on this pretty walk.

There are several other interesting and historic towns to the east of Cape Town. The serene little town of Greyton has attracted a colony of artists and some Capetonians have bought houses here which serve as weekend hideaways. The Post House, one of the lovely hotels in the town, was built in 1860 in English-country style.

Worcester, Robertson, Montagu and Swellendam involve slightly longer drives from Cape Town but are well worth the trip. Worcester has a fascinating outdoor museum depicting the history of agriculture in the area; and Robertson, about 160 km from Cape Town, boasts three wine cellars right in the town and an annual display of roses along the traffic island in the main street.

Montagu, slightly east of Robertson, is set within a region of vineyards and fruit farms. It is well known for the natural mineral spring which attracts visitors all year round to its relaxing warm water. Swellendam, slightly further afield, is one the country's oldest settlements. It has been well preserved and many of its buildings have been splendidly restored. Traditional country crafts have been relearned and are carried out in the town's country museum, designed like an old village green.

To the north-east of Cape Town is the historic town of Tulbagh which was hit by an earthquake in 1969. The town has, however, been lovingly restored and contains one of the highest concentrations of national monuments in the country; Church Street is especially noted for its collection of national monuments which numbers some 32 proclaimed buildings. Also of interest is the Tulbagh Museum, housed in the former Dutch Reformed Church.

A favourite day drive from Cape Town is the so-called Four Passes Drive, which follows a route past Somerset West and over Sir Lowry's Pass, through Grabouw and over the spectacular Viljoen's Pass to Theewaterskloof Dam. Franschhoek Pass winds down to the historic Franschhoek valley, dotted with wine farms bearing French names. The last pass is the Helshoogte Pass, now an easy sweep of wide road, having been tamed considerably in recent times. Parts of the tortuously twisting original pass can still be seen along the way. This route finally takes the traveller into Stellenbosch, probably just in time for a well-earned glass of local wine after the 200-km-drive.

The western Cape is not all craggy mountain passes, however, and to the north of Cape Town lies a very different drive. The long West Coast road leads through wide open country to Langebaan, a birdwatchers paradise where around 55 000 birds make their home in summer. The shallow, sheltered lagoon here also attracts windsurfers and small watercraft, and is surrounded by safe bathing beaches. The National Parks Board runs the excellent hotel here. On the other side of the lagoon is a long peninsula which contains the Postberg nature reserve, offering some game and a riot of colourful wild flowers every spring, and the tiny fishing village of Churchhaven.

A little further along the coast is Saldanha Bay, with a busy fishing harbour and ore-loading terminal. Many Cape yachtsmen, tired of the oily pollution and high cost of keeping their boats in Table Bay, have moorings at Saldanha Bay Yacht Club and travel to the town every weekend for their sailing. This is an area of low shrubland, with few trees and no mountains. The soil is chalky white and the climate hot and dry.

But the rugged coast is relatively unspoilt and the fishing villages such as St Helena Bay, Velddrif, Paternoster and Stompneusbaai have a primitive charm of their own. There is little here to tempt the five-star traveller, but for anybody wanting to get away from it all, the West Coast undoubtedly fits the bill.

The little farming town of Tulbagh, once devastated by an earthquake, has been restored and now has one of the greatest concentrations of declared historic monuments in the Cape.

LEFT: *Visitors to the summit of Table Mountain stare in awe as foggy fingers of mist creep into the deep valleys between the peaks of the Twelve Apostles. The erratic weather pattern of the Cape Peninsula means that the vista from the mountain can change from hour to hour.*

ABOVE: *Built of the same sandstone on which it stands, the alpine-style restaurant on the top of Table Mountain plays host to thousands of visitors annually.*

RIGHT: *Another car-load of visitors eases its way into the docking bay at the upper cable station. The precarious-looking exposed platform on top of the car carries an inspector up and down every day. The unbroken safety record must be maintained!*

LEFT: *Surrounded by awe-inspiring rocky ramparts and brightly coloured wild flowers, a hiker strides out along the Saddle Path across the face of Table Mountain. Walking on the mountain is recommended only for the experienced, or in the company of a competent guide. The upper cable station can be seen at the far right.*

BELOW LEFT: *Apprehensive passengers take a last nervous look back at the lower cable station as they begin the soaring ride to the mountain's summit. Some love it. Others close their eyes and wait for it to end. But the view from the top, more than 1 000 metres above the sea, is worth every minute.*

RIGHT: *The towering pinnacle of Lion's Head to the right stands guard over Kloof Nek, the mountain gap that links Cape Town to Camp's Bay. Signal Hill, from which this photograph was taken, is a favourite viewing point that offers a panoramic view of the city bowl and Table Bay on the one side, and Sea Point on the other.*

TOP: *High above the city, visitors to the summit of Table Mountain study the geography of the Peninsula. The relief map enables visitors to orientate themselves in this confusing part of the Cape.*

ABOVE: *The strong hands of the south-easter prepare to spread the tablecloth over the mountain. Legend has it that this 'cloth' is the result of a furious, centuries-old smoking contest between Van Hunks and the devil.*

ABOVE: *The restaurant at the top of Table Mountain provides a welcome stop for energetic climbers who have come up the hard way – on foot. For most, however, it's the room with the view – certainly one of the most spectacular in the world. From the walled area below the restaurant the vista stretches forever, over the rocky buttresses of the Twelve Apostles, down to Cape Point and far across the restless south Atlantic.*

LEFT: *Many kilometres of winding pathways make Table Mountain a favourite haunt of hikers. Here, flanked by protea bushes and mountain flora, the walker is offered a stunning view of the majestic Lion's Head peak. Other mountain visitors, less energetic, enjoy the same view from the cable car overhead.*

TOP RIGHT: *While many of the wild animals that once lived on the Peninsula have long since vanished, the dassie or rock rabbit, that unlikely relative of the elephant, thrives and multiplies on the rocky slopes of Table Mountain. These charming little creatures have become quite unafraid of humans and regard them with calm curiosity.*

RIGHT: *A wealth of delicate mountain blooms greets the springtime hiker at every turn. Ruled by the stately proteas,the Cape's floral kingdom contains hundreds of varieties of wild flowers from bold pelargoniums to fragile watsonias shown here.*

BOTTOM RIGHT: *The red disa, known as the Pride of Table Mountain, is a strictly protected member of the orchid family.*

OPPOSITE: *The twin spires of the oldest synagogue in South Africa, situated in the Company's Garden (commonly known as the Gardens) at the top end of Adderley Street, glow in the evening sun. The synagogue is now the Jewish Museum which depicts the history of the Jewish people in South Africa and contains a unique collection of Jewish ceremonial items.*

ABOVE: *This energetic and vibrant equestrian statue tops a war memorial in front of the South African Museum. Popular features of the museum include the whale well and planetarium.*
RIGHT: *Rough and rugged, this controversial statue of General Jan Smuts in the Gardens caused such an uproar when it was unveiled that a new and more realistic one was erected at the top end of Adderley Street.*

JAN CHRISTIAN
SMUTS

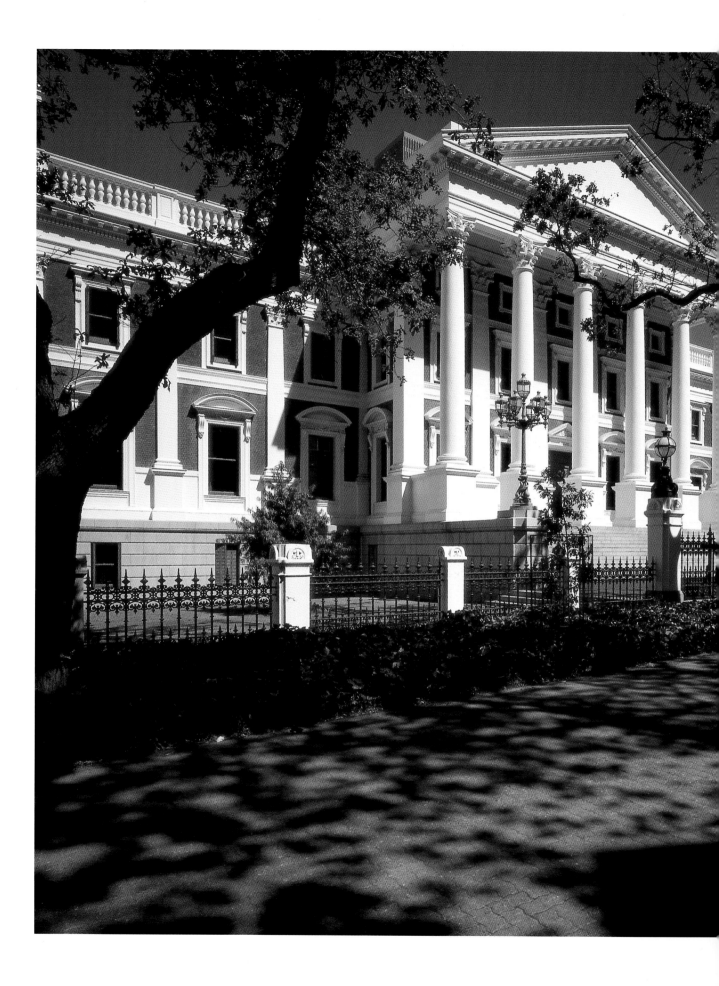

LEFT: *Cape Town is the legislative capital of South Africa and it is in the Houses of Parliament, situated beside the Gardens, that the country's often controversial laws have been made – and unmade. With the country in a state of political change, the role of Parliament is likely to alter dramatically in the next few years.*

ABOVE: *The Gardens provide a welcome refuge from the hustle and bustle of modern city life. It was originally started as a vegetable garden to provide fresh produce for the settlers and crews of visiting vessels, and is now an interesting botanic garden containing plants from many countries.*

BELOW: *For some, the oak-lined Government Avenue is just the shortest way to walk to work. For others, it is a place to escape from the pressures of work for a while during lunch hour. Apart from providing a convenient short cut, the avenue is lined with places of cultural interest like the South African Museum, the Jewish Museum, the National Art Gallery and the South African Library.*

FAR LEFT: *The traffic circles on Cape Town's main street, Adderley Street, feature statues of some of the early pioneers in the Cape. In the foreground Vasco da Gama stares out across the passing traffic. Further up the street Jan van Riebeeck and his wife, Maria, gaze at the city they founded.*

ABOVE: *The Adderley Street flower market provides a splash of bright colour to the city centre and flower sellers entertain passersby with a continual flow of laughter and repartee.*

LEFT: *The cry of the fruit vendor is almost as much a part of Cape Town life as the mountain. 'Loverly bananas, five for a rand', and there's always time to chat to a satisfied customer.*

TOP: *Warm summer evenings are given a touch of fairyland magic by the shimmering Christmas lights a welcome annual feature in Cape Town. Each year residents wait eagerly to see what new illuminations have been dreamed up. Many parents from the suburbs and surrounding towns treat their children to a special trip to Adderley Street during the festive season to 'see the lights'.*

ABOVE: *The setting sun throws Table Mountain into stark silhouette and the bright lights of the big city start to wink their nocturnal messages.*

ABOVE: *From the slopes of Signal Hill the evenings present a glittering carpet of jewels that stretches as far as the eye can see, showing the extent of the sprawling metropolis. Only the sea is dark, save for the gliding lights of passing ships.*

ABOVE: *Cape Town's St George's Cathedral in Wale Street was designed by Sir Herbert Baker and built of Table Mountain sandstone. The building was started in 1901 on the site of an earlier church, but the most recent addition, an octagonal bell tower, was added only in 1980. Apart from the usual church services held at the Cathedral, it is well known for its regular and inspiring performances of sacred music.*

ABOVE: *Long Street contains many attractively restored Victorian shops and office buildings and offers a wealth of interesting little shops selling anything from used clothing to computers.*

FAR LEFT AND LEFT: *In typical Cape Town style, quaint old commercial buildings mix happily with modern multi-storeyed blocks. Visitors to the city are often delighted to discover almost hidden statues and sculptures adorning the older façades.*

Cape Town's Grand Parade can claim the title of South Africa's oldest flea-market. Originally used as a military parade ground, it is now officially a parking area, but most Capetonians know it as the bargain-hunters' mecca. Under the benign façade of the old City Hall, street traders have offered their wares for many decades. The parade's permanent stalls sell fresh fruit and vegetables all week long. On Wednesdays and Saturdays vendors set up temporary stalls where shoppers can find anything from bicycles and cheap jewellery to hot dogs and baby clothes. Probably the most sought-after items are the rolls of inexpensive fabric offered in a rainbow of bright and tempting colours.

OPPOSITE: *For more than three centuries the gateway to the Castle has welcomed the rich, the famous and the powerful. Today streams of tourists pass through South Africa's oldest building to study the collections of art, antiques and military artifacts on display inside.*

ABOVE: *The late afternoon sun drops behind the steeple of the stately Metropolitan Methodist Church and casts long shadows across Greenmarket Square. The old Town House, built in 1755, and* now a repository of old Dutch and Flemish masters, glows crisply white in the evening light. The square is a hive of busy trading during the day, but now the market stalls are packed away for the night, the shoppers have gone and the cobbled square is left to a solitary pigeon.

LEFT: *The doorway to the Methodist Church, built in 1871, is decorated in Gothic Revivalist style. As in all modern cities, pollution and corrosion have taken their toll.*

Surrounded by gracious old buildings, the colourful kaleidoscope of Greenmarket Square's crowded flea-market presents a never-ending procession of gaudy impressions. It's a bright collage of oddly dressed characters, painted hats and watchful faces, buyers, sellers and bystanders. In one stall a herd of floral elephants parades across a field of embroidered flowers. From an upstairs office window the square is a patchwork quilt of bright sunshades and the air is always filled with the sound of buskers. Here it's fine to browse, even without a cent in your pocket. Looking doesn't cost a thing, and all prices are subject to discussion. Haggling is part of the entertainment. The square that was Cape Town's original market has returned to its intended use.

ABOVE LEFT: *Tribal Africa comes to the city centre as a young dancer struts his stuff for the lunchtime crowd in St George's Mall. Buskers make a good living in the city and anyone who can dance or sing is assured of an audience, and an income.*
ABOVE: *All you need is a brolly and a table, and the* mall becomes your market place. Hawking laws have been relaxed considerably in recent times to encourage informal trading.
OPPOSITE: *Cape Town's flower sellers have added colour to the city's streets for generations and Capetonians have responded by making flowers a regular part of their daily lives.*

OPPOSITE: *An informal outdoor antique market has developed in Church Street, traditional home of the city's best known antique dealers. At the outdoor stalls you may not find a genuine Louis XVI escritoire, but if you are looking for the sort of camera you used as a lad, or a replacement for the ice-bucket you inherited from your parents, this is a good place to start. Victorian jewellery, brass house numbers and polished hinges, old leather suitcases, fading photographs and an endless array of old china are available for the browser. And sometimes there are genuine bargains to be found if you know exactly what you're looking for. For most shoppers, however, the joy of Church Street is in discovering a bit of nostalgia that brings back long-forgotten memories.*

ABOVE: *New Year is Coon Carnival time in Cape Town, when teams of brightly dressed minstrels compete for prizes in traditional music and dancing categories. Thousands of man-hours go into the making of the gaudy satin suits, and each troupe keeps its own design a secret until that opening number.*

LEFT: *The 'flute man' demonstrates a set of pan-pipes. His haunting piping has been heard in the streets of Cape Town for decades. For those who don't buy his wares, he has a lively line in insults!*

ABOVE: *The Bo-Kaap, with its small, but lovingly restored houses, is home to many of Cape Town's Malay families. Here Islam is the dominant religion, and the red fez indicates that the wearer has completed his pilgrimage to Mecca. Several old mosques serve the community, and the chanting of the muezzin from the mosque tower calls the faithful to prayer five times a day. The evening sun catches white-washed walls as three friends pause to chat under the shadow of Table Mountain.*

LEFT: *With few trees to climb in the densely populated Bo-Kaap, a youngster finds great delight in shinning to the top of the street sign outside his home. Some of the streets in the area are still paved with the cobble stones that were laid several generations ago.*

BELOW: *While many of the houses in the Bo-Kaap are simple, whitewashed cottages, some have been turned into exuberant works of folk art with an architectural style all their own. Bright colours are the order of the day in the narrow streets and ornamentation is lavish, running to plaster reliefs, painted pillars, twisted iron railings and fluted columns.*

OPPOSITE: *The turret of a mosque keeps a protective watch over a cluster of colourful houses in one of the narrow cobbled streets of the Bo-Kaap 'Malay Quarter', unchanged above the bustle of the ever-changing city. Many of the little flat-roofed houses date from the 18th century.*

RIGHT: *Young Muslim children chat on the stone steps as they wait for the mezzuin to summon them to prayer from the local mosque tower. Cape Town's Muslim community is a strong and growing one.*

BELOW: *The Malays have a strong business tradition and have long been suppliers of fruit and vegetables to Cape Town's suburbs.*

NEXT PAGE: *The breathtaking view of the Cape Peninsula from the air.*

OPPOSITE: *Yachting has become a popular pastime for those who can afford it, and the Cape's many boatyards are kept busy producing a seemingly endless stream of craft for racing or cruising sailors. Berthing facilities at the Peninsula's yacht clubs are being strained to their limits.*

ABOVE LEFT: *The Royal Cape Yacht Club in Table Bay provides year-round hospitality to yachtsmen and women from all over the world. The yacht club is the starting point of the South Atlantic Race to Rio, widely acknowledged as one of the great ocean races of the world.*

ABOVE RIGHT: *One of the country's fastest growing watersports is power-boating in inflatable dinghies, known locally as 'rubber ducks'. Hundreds of these lively craft take to the sea every weekend, pounding out through the crashing surf and scurrying across Table Bay and False Bay.*

PREVIOUS PAGE: *Diners take advantage of a balmy summer's evening to relax at a Waterfront restaurant, under the shadow of the darkening Table Mountain. Boats are tied up for the night,* the lights flicker on and the evening's activities begin.
ABOVE LEFT: *Work and play go side by side at the Waterfront, and while some of the boats moored alongside the jetty* take trippers on pleasure voyages round the harbour, others are there to do a hard day's work and cargo nets are filled ready to ferry supplies to ships in the bay.

ABOVE: *Cleverly blending the new with the old, the designers of the Victoria and Alfred Water-front project have managed to retain the character of the old harbour. Long before this scheme was even halfway complete, it had become a tourist magnet, attracting thousands of visitors daily. The numbers continue to grow as this ambitious development expands.*

LEFT: *A jazz duo fills the air with soulful sound at the Waterfront. Here entertainment is provided by a year-round variety show of buskers, acrobats, mime artists and magicians. Food stalls abound for those who would rather stroll than sit.*

ABOVE: *The old clock tower at the harbour once contained the harbour-master's office. Today it's a small museum run by the Ship Society.*

OPPOSITE ABOVE: *The spacious and airy Victoria Wharf shopping complex, originally the site of the Union Castle workshops, now contain more than a dozen restaurants, trendy speciality shops, cinemas and a theatre.*

LEFT: *Pleasure craft of all shapes and sizes can always be seen clustered around Bertie's Landing, one of the first waterside pubs to be opened in the V & A Waterfront scheme. The pub was named after one of the Cape's best-known yachtsmen, Bertie Reed.*

TOP: *Mitchell's Brewery at the Waterfront supplies draught beers brewed in the traditional British style as an alternative to the usual South African lagers.*

The brewery was one of the first taverns to open in the new Waterfront development and has become a popular pub-lunch venue.

ABOVE LEFT: *The lights from a giant oil rig are reflected in the still waters of Table Bay Docks. Off-shore oil rigs are regular visitors to the Cape.*

ABOVE: *The water of the harbour takes on a mirror sheen on a calm summer evening at the V & A Waterfront. The busy quayside pubs and shops stay open until late each night. Evening entertainment here includes sunset cruises on Table Bay and dinners on board a floating restaurant.*

RIGHT: *At the heart of the Waterfront is this large, modern hotel in Victorian style, with an attractive shopping mall on the ground floor. The front of the hotel has become the meeting place for visitors, and it is from here that regular buses leave for the city centre. Careful planning has made the Waterfront one of the most easily accessible tourist attractions in the Cape. Careful policing has made it one of the safest.*

BELOW: *A relic of a more leisurely era, the old 'Penny Ferry' still takes passengers slowly across the entrance of the old Victoria and Alfred Basin in Cape Town's harbour. The fee may have gone up since those old penny days, but the speed and efficiency are unchanged. On a peaceful evening at the Waterfront, who cares if the trip takes a little longer? It's all part of the pleasure.*

OPPOSITE: *Informal lunchtime shows are popular at the Waterfront's amphitheatre, and large crowds gather to enjoy their midday snack and watch a show. Sometimes its a well-drilled troupe of Cape 'coon' musicians, and at other times it might be a magician, a classical guitarist or an acrobat. The show goes on in endless variety.*

ABOVE: *Sea Point, on the Atlantic side of the Peninsula, is undoubtedly the most densely populated area of Cape Town. Here skyscraper blocks of sea-front flats stand shoulder to shoulder. Sea Point, the residents say, is not merely a place. It's a way of life.*

OPPOSITE BELOW: *Sunset cruises are always popular in summer, and trippers line the boat's rail to watch the passing lights of the city while residents stop and stare at the passing boat. It's a spectacular scene, whichever way you look at it – from ship or shore.*

RIGHT: *Cheeky pigeons drop in to lunch as a Sea Point resident opens her sandwiches on a promenade bench. Like urban pigeons throughout the world, these have learned that people usually mean free handouts.*

FAR RIGHT: *The country's oldest lighthouse, built at Green Point by Herman Schutte in 1824, is still in use and is probably best known for its mournful foghorn, which booms across Table Bay when the thick sea mist rolls in. Modern shipping relies heavily on electronic guidance systems, but lighthouses once formed the only warning to visiting vessels at night.*

LEFT: *Lights reflected in the sea at Three Anchor Bay add a touch of unreality to the evening. The brooding silhouette of Lion's Head seems to settle restfully while the lights of this flatland twinkle to wakefulness.*

TOP: *Sunset is the signal for the Atlantic side of the Peninsula to burst into life. Restaurant signs begin flashing their neon invitations to evening diners, and music pours out of pubs and clubs, offering a wide variety of nocturnal delights.*

ABOVE: *A group of energetic young people use the last of the fading sunset to finish their sea-front game of volley-ball. As one of the country's most westerly cities, Cape Town has later sunsets than the rest of the country. Visitors are often surprised to find they can swim or play beach tennis until almost nine o'clock on a midsummer's evening.*

OPPOSITE: *A dramatic gull's-eye view of a block of Bantry Bay time-share flats shows bright brollies blossoming on balconies while the Atlantic crashes on the rocks below.*

ABOVE: *Clinging to the steep slopes of Signal Hill, the sea-front flats of Bantry Bay offer some of Cape Town's most spectacular views.*

RIGHT: *The long stretch of shining white sand at Clifton's popular First Beach draws crowds of sun-worshippers every summer's day. Even if the sea here is usually colder than it is in False Bay, there's never a lack of swimmers.*

OPPOSITE: *Some of the most spectacular homes in the world are to be found clinging to the steep cliffs above the seafront at Clifton on the Atlantic side of the Peninsula. Here bathers enjoy a dip in the sparkling water of a private pool while gentle waves caress the sand of a secluded beach only metres away. Who could ask for more than mermaids at the bottom of the garden?*

ABOVE: *Clifton's Fourth Beach attracts the attractive as sun-worshippers soak up the warm Cape sunshine. On summer weekends the air is rich with the perfume of suntan lotion and ice-cream. For those who like to get away from the crowd, there's always a rock to swim to.*

There's never a shortage of occupants for the towering blocks of holiday flats that line the sea-front.

NEXT PAGE: *One of the most attractive swimming beaches on the Atlantic side of the Penin-sula is Camps Bay, with its wide expanse of smooth white sand bounded by great boulders at each end.*

ABOVE: *A golden mantle of bright spring flowers blooms on the mountain slopes high above the seaside residential area of Camps Bay, nestling at the foot of the rugged Twelve Apostles.*

RIGHT: *For those who enjoy life's quieter pleasures, a game of bowls on a summer weekend is a sheer pleasure. Set between the mountains and the sea, the greens could hardly be in a more attractive position.*

RIGHT: *The Cape's varied landscape provides perfect venues for all kinds of outdoor activities. Here a paraglider pilot guides his colourful canopy gently down from the mountain top toward a smooth landing spot on Camps Bay beach.*
BELOW: *Sun-worshippers prefer their leisure at a lower altitude and slower pace and relax under canopies of a different kind on the warm sand at Camps Bay.*

ABOVE: *Set against the steep mountain on the route between Camps Bay and Hout Bay, the designer homes of the wealthy at Llandudno offer unrivalled views across the Atlantic. The sheltered beach has become a favourite spot for sunset picnics, and the nearby car park is the starting point for the walk along the coast to Sandy Bay, the Cape's famous nudist beach.*

TOP AND ABOVE: *Llandudno beach offers a gently sloping stretch of silver sand bordered by massive, smooth boulders. It attracts sea lovers of all ages, whether their interest is surf and bikinis or the serious business of loading treasures on to little lorries. The protected beach, sheltered from the Cape south-easter, offers no hazards more serious than a case of sunburn.*

ABOVE AND RIGHT: *Sheltered by Chapman's Peak to the southeast and the Sentinel to the west, the pretty village of Hout Bay has attracted a busy population of artists and craftspeople. Hout Bay residents have developed a fiercely independent spirit and declared themselves the 'Republic of Hout Bay', only partly in jest. Once a year, at the popular Hout Bay Festival, 'immigration officials' issue passports to visitors and rumour has it that travellers have used these mock passports without trouble in some foreign countries.*

ABOVE AND ABOVE LEFT: *Hout Bay's World of Birds, started by Walter Mangold as a sanctuary for injured birds, has developed into one of the area's major tourist attractions. Unlike most zoos and bird parks, the World of Birds welcomes visitors inside the aviaries with the birds. Many visitors find tranquillity while sitting on the shaded benches surrounded by fearless owls, hawks and other bird species. Here Mr Mangold introduces a greater kestrel to a group of visiting school children, while a cattle egret in breeding plumage preens itself in the foliage.*

LEFT: *Kronendal, an elegant Hout Bay house in traditional Cape Dutch style, was built in the late 18th century, and has been declared a National Monument. In recent years it has served as a restaurant and antiques centre.*

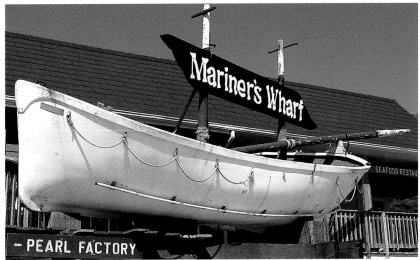

LEFT: *Hout Bay's busy fishing harbour is home to a fleet of trawlers and crayfishing vessels. Factories in the dock area process fresh fish and crayfish for the local and export markets and factory shops sell their fresh wares directly to the public. Once used solely for commercial fishing, the harbour now accommodates a rapidly growing fleet of yachts, and several charter boats take trippers on voyages around the sheltered bay. One of the most popular trips is to nearby Duiker Island to watch the seals at play.*

TOP: *Mariners' Wharf, a quaint quayside emporium, offers seafoods as fresh as the breeze. Some like to take them home while others stay to enjoy the fine view from the restaurant balcony, or to buy a packet of fish and chips to munch while strolling along the seafront.*

ABOVE: *The Chapman's Peak Hotel has become a popular mealtime meeting place and seafood is, of course, the speciality of the house. Here guests enjoy an alfresco meal with a view almost as good as the food.*

PREVIOUS PAGE: *Carved into the solid rock of the mountain, Chapman's Peak Drive curves along the craggy coastline, high above the sea, and is considered to be one of the most spectacular mountain drives in the world. Apart from its scenic attraction, the drive forms part of the route of two of the country's biggest sporting events, the Two Oceans Marathon and the Argus Cycle Tour, both of which attract thousands of entries from all four provinces. Parking spots and picnic sites along the route lure hundreds of sightseers every weekend.*

LEFT: *Noordhoek beach is a favourite spot for surfers when conditions are right. Youngsters enjoy pottering about in the rock pools and the long sweep of white sand is perfect for walkers to exercise their dogs and for horse-riding. At the far end of the beach is the village of Kommetjie.*

ABOVE: *Once just cottages in rather a remote outpost, Kommetjie is now a thriving residential village. The little bay, or 'kom' is a traditional crayfishing spot, inaccessible to any but the smallest boats. Slangkop lighthouse, to the right, is an important aid to passing ships and the local fishing fleet.*

ABOVE: *Flocks of seabirds have the rocky inlet at Olifantsbos- baai in the Cape of Good Hope Nature Reserve all to themselves. From here you can walk to the wreck of the* Thomas T. Tucker.

TOP RIGHT: *Towering high above the ocean, this monument to Vasco da Gama in the Cape of Good Hope Nature Reserve commemorates his historic voyage round the Cape in 1497.*

MIDDLE AND RIGHT: *Pretty pink heather forms a natural carpet of colour, and a curious baboon, one of the most visible animals in the nature reserve, keeps an eye on visitors.*

ABOVE: *The rocky Cape of Storms points a warning finger at passing ships. Whatever the atlas may say, Capetonians are convinced that this is the true meeting place of the two oceans. This unspoiled tip of the Peninsula has been declared a nature reserve and is home to several species of buck and other animals. The lighthouse here is one of the most powerful in the world.*

RIGHT: *A small herd of bontebok interrupt their grazing to watch the photographer alertly. There are eight species of buck in the reserve, as well as ostriches, baboons and many smaller mammals, birds and reptiles.*

FAR RIGHT: *In early spring the Cape Peninsula bursts into colour and one of the world's richest floral kingdoms comes into bloom. The flowers of the West Coast may offer the best massed displays of wild flowers, but the Cape of Good Hope Nature Reserve certainly does not lack variety.*

ABOVE: *Bright oilskins protect rock anglers from the flying spray in the Cape of Good Hope Nature Reserve.*

LEFT: *Dwarfed by the high cliffs of Cape Point, little fishing craft hurry to join the action as news of a good shoal is passed from boat to boat. While there is a small fleet of professional fishing craft based in False Bay, most of the weekend fishing is done from privately owned ski-boats.*

Sometimes the catch is good enough to yield a small profit; at other times it represents a financial loss. The real reason for fishing, however, is to be out on the sea these fishermen love.

ABOVE AND RIGHT: *The Cape of Good Hope Nature Reserve offers some fine fishing waters. Here a group of divers prepares for a morning of spear-fishing, and a successful fisherman proudly displays his catch.*

ABOVE: *Sightseers gaze down at the southernmost tip of the Peninsula from the lofty lookout platform on the peak of Cape Point. Passing ships give this turbulent meeting place of currents a wide berth.*

RIGHT: *Close to the tip of the Cape Peninsula is this sheltered little beach known as Diaz Beach, not much used by bathers or picnickers simply because of the steep access paths down the rocky cliffs.*

ABOVE: *A white-breasted cormorant, an efficient underwater hunter, eyes the sea from his solid rocky perch.*
RIGHT: *Probably the most exclusive holiday resort in the country, Smitswinkel Bay is inaccessible by road. Every bit of material required to build the small cluster of weekend cottages had to be carried down the steep cliff path. Residents park at the roadside, high above the bay, and clamber down for their regular escape from the hustle and hassle of modern life. Once ensconced in their secure hideaways, they can be sure of a weekend uninterrupted by any visitors apart from an occasional yacht which might anchor in the sheltered bay for an afternoon of swimming or fishing.*

OPPOSITE: *Rolling green lawns reach almost to the water's edge at the sheltered Seaforth Beach at Simon's Town. Swimming is safe and there are nearby rocks for sunbathing.*

ABOVE: *A bobbing flotilla of small craft fills the historic Simon's Bay, traditional head-quarters of the South African Navy. The village has a long naval tradition and has retained its naval character.*

RIGHT: *The buildings along Simon's Town's main street have been carefully restored to their Victorian splendour. Each façade along this 'historic mile' has an interesting story to tell. Once part of the town's links with the Navy, they now house shops and restaurants.*

OPPOSITE TOP: *Silvery snoek are the economic lifeblood of the little fishing village of Kalk Bay. Eager buyers line the jetty to bid for the day's shining harvest as fish are tossed ashore to be bought, sold and probably sold again.*

OPPOSITE FAR LEFT: *Unlike Hout Bay across the Peninsula, where there are large fleets of commercial fishing vessels,*

Kalk Bay is home to a motley collection of individually owned line boats. Although the living is precarious, each boat owner is his own boss. The craft are carefully tended and painted in proud primary colours.

OPPOSITE LEFT: *Where there are working boats, there are always seafaring characters to be found, burned by the sun and bleached by the salt of the sea.*

ABOVE: *Trek fishing boats, their nets piled ready in their sterns, rest on the white sand at Fish Hoek beach. This delightful little bay is popular with bathers of all ages, and some hardy swimmers come for an early morning dip every day, even in the middle of winter. The trek fishing boats provide an added attraction when the fish are running.*

PREVIOUS PAGE: *Bright bathing huts glow in the morning sunlight before bathers arrive at St James's pool. Once the preserve of the rich, St James has become a well-used family beach, boasting large crowds on weekends and holidays.*
LEFT: *There's room for everyone on the long, gentle sweep of Muizenberg beach. The west end attracts weekend surfers, the bathers have several kilometres of sea to themselves, while the surf anglers stick to the remote unspoiled stretches to the east.*
ABOVE: *Muizenberg Pavilion provides entertainment for all, including a putt-putt course.*

117

LEFT: *Klein Constantia, once part of Simon van der Stel's original farm, has been renovated and turned into one of the most modern and successful wineries in the Cape. But on the surface, time has passed it by and cows graze on soft green pastures in front of the old manor house as they have done for three centuries. The cellar is open for tastings and wine sales.*
ABOVE: *The fine restored manor house at Groot Constantia is a good example of Cape Dutch architecture, with its ornate white gable and small-paned sash windows. The farm was established in 1685, and the house rebuilt a century later. It was destroyed by fire in 1925 and has been carefully restored to its present grandeur.*

ABOVE: *On fine summer days guests at the Jonkershuis Restaurant at Groot Constantia enjoy a meal of traditional Cape fare in the shade of the spreading oaks. The Jonkershuis is one of two restaurants on the estate.*

RIGHT: *The Groot Constantia manor house, now a museum, provides an accurate record of early life at the Cape, with each of the rooms carefully furnished according to the period. In this airy dining room the gleaming clay tiles of the floor reflect the rich patina of fine handcrafted furniture, polished regularly for more than a century.*

RIGHT BELOW: *An elegantly turned and carved four-poster is the focal point of this bedroom in the Groot Constantia manor house. The suspended cradle is a splendid example of fine craftmanship and has probably held many generations of babies.*

ABOVE AND LEFT: *Situated near the entrance to Groot Constantia, the Old Cape Farm Stall has become a favourite shopping place for gourmets. Here you can buy crisp fresh fruit and vegetables, flowers, home-baked biscuits and cakes, country preserves and many other rural delicacies – all within a few minutes' drive from the centre of the city. The farm stall also offers delicious breakfasts, teas and lunches, prepared from fresh farm produce.*

ABOVE: *The Alphen Winery, in the grounds of the gracious Alphen Hotel in Constantia, is now the headquarters of the country's largest wine club, the Wine-of-the-Month Club, with thousands of members in South Africa and abroad. From these premises the distinctive barrel-shaped vans deliver fine Cape wines to wine-lovers all over the Peninsula.*

RIGHT: *Sheltered among the tall trees of the Constantia valley, Buitenverwachting has been restored and turned into a model wine farm. Apart from producing fine wines in an elegant and austere style, the farm is famed for its elegant restaurant. A feature of Buiten-verwachting is the ultra-modern wine cellar, cleverly designed to blend harmoniously with the existing Cape Dutch buildings.*

OPPOSITE: *One of the most renowned botanic gardens in the world, Kirstenbosch, on the eastern slope of Table Mountain, provides a year-round display of the glories of the Cape Floral Kingdom. Meandering paths take visitors on walks along the slopes of the mountain and special features include a fragrance garden and braille trail for the blind, both with explanatory notices in braille.*

ABOVE: *Dappled shade provides a tranquil setting as visitors to Kirstenbosch enjoy a peaceful walk through the Cape flora.*

ABOVE LEFT: *South Africa's national flower, the protea is found in abundance on the slopes of Table Mountain.*

BELOW LEFT: *Clusters of pretty pink ericas offer their tempting nectar to the jewel-bright sun-birds that are attracted by the colourful blooms.*

LEFT: *Appropriately, this vibrant equestrian statue at the Rhodes Memorial on the slopes of Devil's Peak, is called 'Physical Energy'. Much of the land surrounding the memorial was left to the nation by Cecil John Rhodes.*

BELOW: *In the morning mist deer graze among the stone pines near Rhodes Memorial. The deer have become quite tame and often approach visitors to nibble at gifts of bread crusts or lettuce leaves. The view from here across the Cape Flats to the Hottentots-Holland mountains is impressive.*

RIGHT: *Designed by Sir Herbert Baker, this Doric-style temple with its imposing guard of honour of bronze lions is an appropriate memorial to Rhodes, whose vision of a single British colony from the Cape to the equator was never realised. The inscription below the bust of Rhodes was written by his life-long friend, Rudyard Kipling. Behind the memorial is a cosy tearoom.*

ABOVE AND RIGHT: *The wide flight of granite steps to the Jameson Hall is the imposing focal point of the campus of the University of Cape Town, South Africa's oldest university. The university has been a champion of human rights and the 'Jammie steps' have been the meeting place and outdoor debating forum for generations of students. The hall is the venue for important university functions, such as graduation ceremonies.*

OPPOSITE: *Mostert's Mill, just below the University of Cape Town on De Waal Drive, is the only wind-operated mill still in existence in the Cape. It has been restored to full working order and is open to visitors daily. Sybrandt Mostert, the original owner, owned a farm that stretched down to the bank of the Liesbeek River.*

LEFT: *Several attractive, modern seaside playgrounds, like this one near Mitchell's Plain, have been developed along the great sweep of the False Bay coast. Here families can enjoy their weekend outings in supervised safety. There's plenty of parking and the beach is ideal for swimming or surfing.*

BELOW LEFT: *The Cape's rapidly expanding population is being catered for by housing developments such as this on the wide expanse of the Cape Flats. The new residential areas are linked to the city by broad, straight highways, and are close to the sea for weekend recreation. But in spite of all the rapid development, the population growth stays one step ahead.*

RIGHT: *The wide, flat area between Table Mountain and the mountains of the 'Boland' and Stellenbosch has seen many changes. Until quite recently it was almost uninhabited, apart from a few vegetable farmers. Now it is fast being covered by residential development, some of it ordered and neat – other parts a bewildering maze of shacks erected along sandy roads.*

LEFT: *Winemaking was one of the Cape's earliest industries and its products continue to give pleasure to millions of wine-lovers at home and abroad. The wine industry is one of the economic giants of the Western Cape, providing employment and homes to many thousands of farm workers. Enterprising wine farmers have managed to turn what was once simply an agricultural pursuit into a major tourist attraction. Elegant mountain vineyards like these at Stellenzicht lure crowds of visitors to the Cape's many wine routes annually.*

ABOVE: *One of the first signs of spring in the Cape are the punnets of juicy red strawberries at roadside farm stalls. Many women find temporary employment as pickers during the long strawberry season. Old clothes find a new use as colourful uniforms for the many scarecrows, which are a lively and amusing feature of the Stellenbosch strawberry farms.*

ABOVE: *The Oude Libertas Amphitheatre opposite the cellars of the Stellenbosch Farmers' Winery is the setting for a wide variety of musical and dramatic presentations during the summer months. A favourite outing includes a picnic supper on the rolling lawns, followed by an evening of entertainment. The mood is always relaxed and informal, and the wine flows freely at intermission.*

OPPOSITE BELOW: *For thousands of visitors to the Cape each summer, the highlight of the holiday is a day of leisurely tasting in the winelands. The establishment of several wine routes has made wine knowledge readily available to all.*

LEFT: *The pubs and restaurants of Stellenbosch concentrate, naturally, on introducing guests to the fine wines of the region, and are an important feature of student life. Many offer wine tastings and all are ready to offer suggestions and recommend a good wine to go with the dish that's chosen. De Akker is one of the town's most popular drinking spots, and once won the title of Pub of the Year.*

BELOW: *Warm summer evenings find guests enjoying the peace of a glass of wine on the terrace outside a lighted tavern. Wine is the lifeblood of Stellenbosch and very much a part of daily life in this historic town.*

LEFT: *One of the many historic monuments in the old town of Stellenbosch, the Burger Huis is now a museum depicting life in the town in a more leisurely age.*
BELOW LEFT: *This woman in period costume adds a touch of authenticity to the town's Village Museum, a collection of historic buildings that allows the visitor to make a journey through the past, starting from the humblest, through eras of increasing prosperity and sophistication.*
RIGHT: *One of the gems of Stellenbosch is this general dealer's store in Dorp Street. Oom Samie se Winkel seems to have been frozen in time. The prices may have soared, but the goods and the aromas are the same as they were in grand-dad's day. Here you can buy a hand-plaited whip or a roll of chewing tobacco, a jar of home-made chutney, a sturdy basket or a lovingly crocheted table cloth. In Stellenbosch you not only step back into the past, you can buy a piece of it to take home with you.*

LEFT: *Nobody can be surprised that walking is a popular pastime in the Cape. The region is rich in spectacular mountain scenery and shady forest walks. On any of them the beautiful Cape unfolds as a new and exciting vista round every bend. Great care has been taken to create hiking routes that display the Cape at its best without disturbing the environment.*
BELOW: *Life moves at a rather leisurely pace inStellenbosch, and there's always time to take a break from the business of the day for a cup of coffee on the shaded stoep of a pavement restaurant.*

ABOVE: *Stellenbosch is a town of memories and wine, and the two combine in the fascinating Wine Museum in Dorp Street. This huge old wine press stands outside the museum in the grounds of the Distillers' Corporation headquarters. The museum contains priceless articles related to wine, from ancient amphorae and early glass bottles, to ornate corkscrews and decanters.*

ABOVE: *The old Kruithuis, or powder magazine, alongside Die Braak, Stellenbosch's village green, was completed in 1777 to store the arms and ammunition of the Dutch East India Company. Like many of the town's historic buildings, it has been declared a national monument and today houses a small military museum.*

RIGHT: *One of the highest concentrations of national monuments in the country can be found here in Stellenbosch's oak-lined Dorp Street. Almost every building along the street bears a bronze plaque marking it as a national monument. The ornate filigree work on this old house's balcony is typical of buildings of the Victorian era and is known locally as 'broekie lace' (pantie lace). An interesting relic of the past is the water furrow on each side of the street, which once carried the main supply of water to the houses here.*

Focal point of the little town of
Franschhoek, tucked away at
the head of a spectacular valley
to the east of Stellenbosch, is
this monument to the French
Huguenots, who came to the
Cape between 1688 and 1690.
The central figure holds a Bible
in the one hand and a broken
chain in the other, symbolising
freedom from the religious persecution from which they fled.
Alongside the monument is the
Huguenot Museum devoted
to those French pioneers who
established prosperous wine
farms here and founded a wine
industry based on the old French
traditions. The French culture
remains strong today. Many of
the Franschhoek farms still have
French names, and the wines
are made in a style that is close
to that of France.

OPPOSITE TOP AND ABOVE: *Now the property of the giant Anglo American Corporation, Boschendal Estate has been restored to its former glory and has become an extremely popular destination for visitors from all over the world. The farm offers diners meals in one the country's best-known restaurants, or superb picnic lunches under towering pines. Boschendal wines have earned an enviable reputation internationally. The manor house, dating from 1812, is now a museum, open to the public.*

OPPOSITE MIDDLE: *The pretty little town of Franschhoek has become known for its fine restaurants and unhurried pace. Here diners take a leisurely break on the veranda of an informal coffee shop.*

OPPOSITE BELOW: *Franschhoek has also become known for its art and craft shops and there are several galleries like this one offering fine work for sale.*

ABOVE: *The original farming settlement of Paarl, founded in 1720, is now a sprawling town, closely linked to the wine industry. There are several hectares of vineyards right in the middle of the village, and the KWV, governing body of the Cape wine industry, has its headquarters here.*

RIGHT: *Early morning dew glistening on these towering rocks on the hilltop overlooking the town gave Paarl its name – the Pearl.*

ABOVE: *The beautiful, gabled homestead at Nederburg, near Paarl, is set on one of the best-known wine farms in the country, and is the venue for an annual auction of rare and valuable wines.*

LEFT: *Fresh farm produce is available all year round at the Cape and the countryside is dotted with cheerful little farm stalls like this one between Stellenbosch and Paarl.*

OPPOSITE TOP: *All rigged up and somewhere to go. Colourful catamaran sails flutter in the breeze as sailors prepare to slip through the surf on the beach at Strand, a popular resort on the eastern side of False Bay, where the ride is wet and wild.*

OPPOSITE BELOW: *Fishing becomes a family sport on the beach, and the morning sun warms bathers and dissolves the mist to reveal the mountains surrounding the Strand. The long stretches of white, sun-kissed sand are perfect for all sorts of seaside activities.*

ABOVE: *The evening tide ebbs and the sky turns to copper as diners settle down to a romantic meal in this Strand restaurant built right out over the sea. Many of the hotels and restaurants along the False Bay coast provide guests with unsurpassed views of the sea and mountains.*

ABOVE LEFT: *Gordon's Bay, to the south-east of Strand on the False Bay coast, was once just a small fishing village. It is now home to a fleet of elegant modern cruising yachts and the harbour boasts one of the finest yacht clubs in the Cape.*

ABOVE: *The little shop on the Gordon's Bay harbour once catered only for day trippers. Today it serves the yachting fraternity as well.*

LEFT: *For some, the harbour wall at Gordon's Bay is an ideal spot for casting lines into the sea. With the sun warming you and the spectacular scenery, who cares whether the fish are biting?*

OPPOSITE: *Set against the craggy backdrop of the rocky mountain, Gordon's Bay is a tiny jewel of a seaside village that has only recently been 'discovered' by the affluent. Today elegant and costly homes are being built on the mountainside and the harbour is filling with modern pleasure craft. But much of its sleepy old-world charm remains.*

ABOVE: *Poised like an eagle about to swoop, this hang-glider prepares to soar over the pretty holiday resort town of Hermanus, just an hour from Cape Town by car. Walker Bay, in the back-ground, is the meeting place of families of whales, who gather in the sheltered waters each spring to mate and calve.*
OPPOSITE TOP: *The old harbour at Hermanus, now a museum, reflects the tough conditions under which the early fishing industry of the town was found-ed. The restored wooden boats drawn up on the concrete slipway will never set out to sea again.*

ABOVE: *Tea is a leisurely affair in one of the popular restaurants in Hermanus, with the sun-warmed tables providing a spectacular view across Walker Bay.*

TOP AND ABOVE: *With its typical rough callosities, a southern right whale surfaces in Walker Bay. These gentle giants attract thousands of visitors to Hermanus every spring. Taking full advantage of the tourist potential of the annual whale visit, the Hermanus town council has appointed a whale crier, who sounds his kelp horn when the whales are sighted, and carries a board giving news about the best viewing sites.*

ABOVE: *The rocky coastline below Hermanus provides scant shelter for boats or bathers, which could be why the bay attracts whales. Further along the coast, however, there's sheltered bathing and small-craft sailing in the lagoon.*

PREVIOUS PAGE: *The West Coast of the Cape is largely undeveloped and unspoiled, but for those who know the area, it has a peace and charm all its own. Churchhaven on the Langebaan Lagoon attracts only a handful of visitors each year. Those who know the spot like to keep the secret to themselves. Nearby is the Postberg nature reserve, known for its spectacular displays of spring flowers.*

OPPOSITE, ABOVE AND NEXT PAGE: *In their brightly painted cockle-shell craft, fishermen at Paternoster put to sea to lay and inspect their rock-lobster traps. The folk who live in the white-washed cottages in this tiny West Coast settlement make their living entirely from the sea, supplying restaurants and hotels throughout the country with these costly crustaceans. The bright colouring*

of the little boats is not mere decoration, as the sea can quickly turn nasty here and it may become necessary to search for lost crews. But the smiles are broad when the harvest is good, and the hard times are quickly forgotten. The robust spirit of the West Coast is typified in the village's hotel, which attracts diners from far and near and sports a rather 'individual' style of decor.

INDEX

Alphabetical order is word-by-word. Page references in italic refer to photographs.